International Investment Law and Gender Equality

AF694827

This book analyses the impact that stabilization clauses have on the development of human rights and gender laws in resource rich nations.

Given the fact that stabilization clauses freeze the law for as long as the contract subsists there has been debate on the negative impact stabilization clauses have on the progressive development of human rights in the host State. Firstly, the book examines the mechanisms investors utilise in protecting themselves from host State prerogatives. It then explores the theoretical basis on which stabilization clauses are applied and upheld by arbitral tribunals, and assesses how they can be drafted in a way that protects human rights, particularly in relation to gender discrimination, without forcing the resource rich nations to lose momentum in attracting foreign direct investment. Using Zambia and the Gender Equity and Equality Act of 2015 as a case study, the book explores the compatibility of the legislation with the stabilization clauses contained in the country's Development Agreements.

The book will be of interest to practitioners, scholars and students of international investment law, human rights law and contract law.

Sangwani Patrick Ng'ambi serves as Lecturer of Law at the University of Zambia. He specialises in Agricultural Law, Contracts, Torts, International Trade Law and International Investment Law.

Kangwa-Musole George Chisanga is a Lecturer of Law at the National Institute for Public Administration. He specialises in International Investment Law, Mining Law and Gender Law.

Routledge Research in International Economic Law

Cohesion and Legitimacy in International Investment Law
Public International Law and Global Administrative Law Perspectives
Chisomo Kapulula

International Challenges in Investment Law and Arbitration
Edited by Mesut Akbaba and Giancarlo Capurro

State Interest and the Sources of International Law
Doctrine, Morality, and Non-Treaty Law
Markus P. Beham

Trade Facilitation in the Multilateral Trading System
Genesis, Course and Accord
Hao Wu

Asian Perspectives on International Investment Law
Edited by Junji Nakagawa

Cost and EU Public Procurement Law
Life-Cycle Costing for Sustainability
Edited by Marta Andhov, Roberto Caranta and Anja Wiesbrock

Promoting and Managing International Investment
Towards an Integrated Policy Approach
Edited by J Anthony VanDuzer and Patrick Leblond

International Investment Law and Gender Equality
Stabilization Clauses and Foreign Investment
Sangwani Patrick Ng'ambi and Kangwa-Musole George Chisanga

For more information about this series, please visit https://www.routledge.com/Routledge-Research-in-International-Economic-Law/book-series/INTECONLAW

International Investment Law and Gender Equality

Stabilization Clauses and Foreign Investment

Sangwani Patrick Ng'ambi and Kangwa-Musole George Chisanga

Routledge
Taylor & Francis Group
LONDON AND NEW YORK

First published 2020
by Routledge
2 Park Square, Milton Park, Abingdon, Oxon OX14 4RN

and by Routledge
605 Third Avenue, New York, NY 10017

First issued in paperback 2021

Routledge is an imprint of the Taylor & Francis Group, an informa business

© 2020 Sangwani Patrick Ng'ambi and Kangwa-Musole George Chisanga

The right of Sangwani Patrick Ng'ambi and Kangwa-Musole George Chisanga to be identified as authors of this work has been asserted by them in accordance with sections 77 and 78 of the Copyright, Designs and Patents Act 1988.

All rights reserved. No part of this book may be reprinted or reproduced or utilised in any form or by any electronic, mechanical, or other means, now known or hereafter invented, including photocopying and recording, or in any information storage or retrieval system, without permission in writing from the publishers.

Trademark notice: Product or corporate names may be trademarks or registered trademarks, and are used only for identification and explanation without intent to infringe.

Publisher's Note
The publisher has gone to great lengths to ensure the quality of this reprint but points out that some imperfections in the original copies may be apparent.

British Library Cataloguing-in-Publication Data
A catalogue record for this book is available from the British Library

Library of Congress Cataloging-in-Publication Data
Names: Ng'ambi, Sangwani Patrick, author. | Chisanga, Kangwa-Musole George, author.
Title: International investment law and gender equality: stabilization clauses and foreign investment/Sangwani Patrick Ng'ambi and Kangwa-Musole George Chisanga.
Description: Abingdon, Oxon; New York, NY: Routledge, 2020. | Series: Routledge research in international economic law | Includes bibliographical references and index.
Identifiers: LCCN 2019058919 (print) | LCCN 2019058920 (ebook)
Subjects: LCSH: Investments, Foreign (International law)—Social aspects. | Women—Legal status, laws, etc. | Investments, Foreign—Law and legislation—Zambia. | Women—Legal status, laws, etc.—Zambia.
Classification: LCC K3830 .N43 2020 (print) | LCC K3830 (ebook) | DDC 346/.0922—dc23
LC record available at https://lccn.loc.gov/2019058919
LC ebook record available at https://lccn.loc.gov/2019058920

ISBN 13: 978-1-03-223648-3 (pbk)
ISBN 13: 978-0-367-07596-5 (hbk)

DOI: 10.4324/9780429021480

Typeset in Galliard
by codeMantra

This book is dedicated to Justice Mulela M. Munalula of the Constitutional Court of Zambia, for inspiring a generation of scholars in gender and the law

Contents

1 Introduction 1

2 The doctrine of permanent sovereignty over natural resources 17

3 Political risk and the effect of stabilization clauses in concession agreements 45

4 Stabilization clauses and human rights concerns 78

5 Stabilization clauses and gender equality: a case study of Zambia 99

6 Conclusion 125

Bibliography 129
Index 137

1 Introduction

1.1 Introduction

Foreign Direct Investment essentially involves the transfer of tangible or intangible assets from one jurisdiction to the other. The aim of this transfer of assets is to generate wealth. Furthermore, these assets are either totally or partially controlled by the owner.[1] Foreign investment is typically fostered through some kind of agreement between the host State and the foreign investor. In mineral-rich nations, such agreements are called concessions. Such agreements can run for a period of up to thirty years or more.[2]

The signing of such an agreement is meant to be the beginning of a mutually beneficial relationship between the host State and the investor. There are certainly a number of benefits that the host State derives from foreign direct investment. These include inter alia: foreign capital, technical know-how, jobs and access to new technology.[3] The investor, of course, makes a profit from their investment. However, the latter scenario is largely contingent upon the protections afforded to the investor over the period that the concession runs.

International standards for investment protection have evolved tremendously over the past century. Prior to 1945, investment protection was less of a cause for concern.[4] This was owing to the fact that much of the foreign investment was made in the context of colonialism. This essentially meant that investment was going directly from the imperial state to the colonies. The legal systems of the colonies were largely integrated with those of the colonisers. Therefore, protections were typically sufficient.

The period between 1945 and 1990 saw the emergence of newly independent States and the dissolution of the imperial powers. These States not only sought

1 Muthucumaraswamy Sornarajah, *The International Law on Foreign Investment* (3rd edn, Cambridge University Press 2010) 8.

2 Rudolph Dolzer and Christoph Schreuer, *Principles of International Investment Law* (2nd edn, OUP 2012) 21.

3 James C. Baker, *Foreign Direct Investment in Less Developed Countries: The Role of ICSID and MIGA* (Quorum Books 1999) 5.

4 Kenneth J. Vandevelde, "A Brief History of International Investment Agreements" (2005) 12 *University of California Davis Journal of International Law and Policy* 157, 158.

political independence but also sought economic independence. This meant maximizing their control over their natural resources. The theory of permanent sovereignty over natural resources was thus propounded. This is the principle from which newly independent States derived their right to nationalize foreign assets. By the 1990s, however, a slump in natural resource prices and mismanagement led to economic crises in these host States. They thus sought to attract foreign investment. To protect these investments, States also entered into various Bilateral Investment Treaties (BITs), affording protections to foreign investors.

This chapter will provide a comprehensive overview of the system of international investment law. Given the relevance of arbitral case law in the development of investment law, it will offer a first glance at how investment arbitration works. Section 1.7 will give an overview of the chapters of this book.

1.2 The evolution of international investment law

Much of the law relating to foreign direct investment has been developed around the protection afforded to foreign nationals both domestically and under international law. Before the Second World War, however, the protection of foreign direct investments was not typically a cause for concern.[5] This is owing to the fact that foreign direct investment in the eighteenth and nineteenth centuries existed within the context of colonialism.[6] Colonial legal systems were integrated with those of the imperial powers. The protections granted to investment under the imperial legal systems were sufficient. Therefore, the need to protect foreign investors through an international legal system was minimal.

This position was certainly reflected in the treaty practice of the nineteenth century. The protection of investors under treaties relied not on a minimum international standard of protection for foreign investors but rather on domestic laws of the host States. An example of this is found in the 1950 Treaty between Switzerland and the United States. Article 2(3) of the aforementioned Treaty provided that:

> In the case of … expropriation for purposes of public utility, the citizens of one of the two countries, residing or established in the other, shall be placed on an equal footing with the citizens of the country in which they reside in respect to indemnities for damages they may have sustained.[7]

This assumption that the domestic law of the host State would provide sufficient protection to investors was, however, brought into doubt by a concatenation of circumstances. This included the emergence of the Calvo Doctrine, the Russian Revolution and the Mexican nationalizations.

5 Ibid 158.
6 Sornarjah (n 1) 19.
7 cited in Dolzer and Schreuer (n 2) 1.

The Calvo Doctrine was propounded by Carlos Calvo, who was an Argentine jurist. Under this doctrine, international investment disputes must be settled under the jurisdiction in which the investment is located. As such, neither diplomatic protection nor any intervention is to be afforded to a foreign investor, until all local remedies are exhausted. The foreign investor must use the local courts of the home country before seeking some external recourse. This doctrine was certainly incorporated in the constitutions of several Latin American countries. It was also included in several treaties, statutes and contracts. It was particularly utilized in concession agreements. Under such agreements, the local courts were given final jurisdiction.

The Russian Revolution of 1917 occurred subsequently to the emergence of the Calvo Doctrine. During this period, the government of the Soviet Union proceeded to expropriate enterprises belonging to both nationals and non-nationals without compensation. The Soviet Union justified its taking of alien property without compensation by invoking the national treatment standard. These are the circumstances that led to the dispute in *Lena Goldfields v USSR.*[8] In this case, the Soviet government had expropriated assets belonging to Lena Goldfields, in contravention of an agreement not to do so. In this case the tribunal awarded compensation to Lena Goldfields, on the principle of unjust enrichment.

Mexico's nationalization of US interests in its agrarian and oil business gave rise to an opportunity for the development of international investment law. Between 1915 and 1930, Mexico has expropriated various assets belonging to US citizens. These included agricultural lands and petroleum concessions.

Subsequently to these nationalizations, there were lengthy diplomatic exchanges between the US Secretary of State, Cordell Hull, and the Mexican Minister of Foreign Affairs. Writing on 3 August 1938, the Mexican Minister of Foreign Affairs opined that there was no obligation under international law to pay immediate or deferred compensation for "expropriations of a general and impersonal character like those which Mexico has carried out for the purpose of redistribution of the land …"[9] The American government, however, had an alternative view. What was espoused in response has come to be known as the "Hull Principle". Thus, in his response on 22 August, US Secretary of State Cordell Hull asserted that:

> The government of the United States merely adverts to a self-evident fact when it notes that the applicable precedents and recognized authorities on international law support its declaration that, under every rule of law and equity, no government is entitled to expropriate property, for whatever purpose, without provision for prompt, adequate, and effective payment therefor.

8 Arthur Nussbaum, "The Arbitration between the Lena Goldfields, Ltd. and the Soviet Government" (1950–51) *Cornell Law Quarterly* 31, 42.

9 Green Hackworth, *Digest of International Law: Volume 3* (US Government Printing Office 1942) 657.

> In addition, clauses appearing in the constitutions of almost all nations today, and in particular in the constitutions of the American republics, embody the principle of just compensation. These, in themselves, are declaratory of the like principle in the law of nations.[10]

As such, the American government asserted that if a government expropriates property belonging to a foreign national, then this will be subject to prompt, adequate and effective compensation. On the other hand, the Mexican government essentially took a position that was more congruous with the Calvo Doctrine. This clash of ideologies was one that would reoccur globally during the post-colonial period.[11]

The need to have a more comprehensive system of protection for foreign investors was necessitated by the dissolution of empires, which accelerated after the end of the Second World War. Thus, the period between 1945 and 1990 saw the number of newly independent States grow.[12] These States not only sought political independence, they also demanded economic independence. The latter was inextricably linked to greater control over their natural resources for the purposes of economic development.[13] This period therefore saw the birth of the principle of permanent sovereignty over natural resources.

The principle of permanent sovereignty over natural resources essentially espouses that States have the right to do whatsoever they wish with natural resources found in their jurisdiction. This includes the right to enter into concession agreements with foreign investors, thus enabling them to explore and exploit natural resources found within their jurisdiction. It also includes the right to nationalize, provided that the host State pays appropriate compensation to the investor.

This was certainly highlighted in General Assembly Resolution 1803, which was seen as a landmark resolution on permanent sovereignty over natural resources.[14] It recognized, "The right of people's and nations to permanent sovereignty over their wealth and resources must be exercised in the interest of their national development and the well-being of the people of the State concerned".

10 Ibid 658–659.

11 Sornarajah (n 1) 21.

12 Adeoye Akinsanya, "Permanent Sovereignty over Natural Resources and the Future of Foreign Investment" (1978) 7 *Journal of International Studies* 124, 126.

13 Lilian A. Miranda, "The Role of International Law in Intrastate Natural Resource Allocation: Sovereignty, Human Rights, and People-Based Development" (2012) 45 *Vanderbilt Journal of Transnational Law* 785, 794, Andreas R. Ziegler and Louis-Philippe Gratton, "Investment Insurance" in Peter Muchlinski, Federico Ortino and Christoph Schreuer (eds), *The Oxford Handbook of International Investment Law* (OUP 2008) 526

14 General Assembly Resolution 1803 (XVII) of 14 December 1962, See also Marilda Rosado de Sá Ribeiro, "Sovereignty over Natural Resources Investment Law and Expropriation: The Case of Bolivia and Brazil" (2009) 2 *Journal of World Energy Law & Business* 129, 130 and Nico Schrijver, "Natural Resource Management and Sustainable Development" in Thomas G. Weiss and Sam Daws (eds), *The Oxford Handbook on the United Nations* (OUP 2007) 596.

The right to nationalize was contingent on the payment of "appropriate compensation". General Assembly Resolution 1803 was followed by the Charter of Economic Rights and Duties of States (CERDS). It provided that:

> Each State has the right to ... (c) To nationalize, expropriate or transfer ownership of foreign property, in which case appropriate compensation should be paid by the State adopting such measures, taking into account its relevant laws and regulations and all circumstances that the State consider pertinent.[15]

The principle of permanent sovereignty over natural resources became recognized as a legitimate part of customary international law. Thus, in the case of *LIAMCO v Libya*,[16] the arbitrator held that, "the said Resolutions, if not a unanimous source of law, are evidence of the recent dominant trend of international opinion concerning the sovereign right of States over natural resources".[17] Similarly, in *Congo v Uganda*[18] the International Court of Justice recognized permanent sovereignty over natural resources as "a principle of customary international law".[19]

International recognition of the principle of permanent sovereignty over natural resources led to insecurity about the rules relating to the protection of foreign investment. Certainly, the period that followed the introduction of the principle of permanent sovereignty over natural resources saw a number of newly independent States nationalizing assets to foreign investors. This was as a result of newly independent States beginning to reconsider concession agreements formalized prior to independence. A number of these were considered "inequitable and onerous".[20] As such, natural resources were in the hands of State-owned corporations. This period lasted generally until 1990.

15 UN GA Res 3281 (12 December 1974).

16 (1977) 62 ILR 141.

17 *Liamco v Libya* (226) 53, paragraph 100.

18 *Case concerning Armed Activities on the Territory of the Congo (Democratic Republic of the Congo v Uganda)* I.C.J. Reports 2005, p. 168.

19 Paragraph 244. Note however that it does not apply in situations of "looting, pillage and exploitation of certain natural resources by members of the army of a State militarily intervening in another State". Judge Koroma in his declaration contends that the ICJ's acknowledgement of the principle as a customary norm implies that the rights and duties emanating from it, "remain in effect at all times, including *during armed conflict and occupation*" (paragraph 11). This can be contrasted with ad hoc Judge Kateka who said that "The PSNR was adopted in the era of decolonization and the assertion of the rights of newly independent States. It thus would be inappropriate to invoke this concept in a case involving two African countries. This remark is made without prejudice to the right of States to own and or dispose of their natural resources as they wish" (paragraph 56).

20 Subrata Roy Chowdhury, "Permanent Sovereignty over Natural Resources: Substratum of the Seoul Declaration" in Paul de Wart, Paul Peters and Erik Denters (eds), *International Law and Development* (Martinus Nijhoff 1988) 61.

1.3 Foreign investment in the context of modern international law

Nationalization did not bring the much-anticipated prosperity to the people of resource-rich nations. Instead, mismanagement and a reduction in world oil and mineral prices saw the decline of industries in resource-rich nations. In order to resuscitate these industries capital would be needed. In order to raise such capital, host States began to encourage the flow of foreign investment. Host States essentially fostered this through liberalizing their economies and privatizing their oil and mineral companies. This was invariably fostered through concession agreements. In addition to this, to guarantee protection to foreign investors, BITs were signed. These often included various clauses which were antithetical to the Calvo Doctrine. As a result, the Calvo doctrine lost traction after 1990.

This was further accentuated by the Washington Consensus arrived at by international financial institutions. Under this Consensus, the emphasis was on the role of the private sector in the process of development. In their view, encouraging the flow of private foreign investment was a means through which development could be achieved. This was certainly emphasized in the preamble of the World Bank's Guidelines on the Treatment of Foreign Direct Investment, which recognized that:

> a greater flow of foreign direct investment brings substantial benefits to bear on the world economy and on the economies of developing countries in particular, in terms of improving the long term efficiency of the host country through greater competition, transfer of capital, technology and managerial skills and enhancement of market access in terms of the expansion of international trade.[21]

Efforts were also made to ensure that investors were protected from the non-commercial risks associated with foreign direct investment. These risks included nationalization, war and civil disturbance and restrictions on externalization of profits. As such, insurance schemes such as the Multilateral Investment Guarantee Agency (MIGA) were introduced. MIGA operates under the auspices of the World Bank.[22] It was established in 1988 with the aim of encouraging the flow of foreign direct investment to developing countries.[23] It does so under Article 11 of the MIGA Convention by covering various non-business risks. These include nationalization, war or civil disturbance, breach of contract and any losses arising from any restrictions on the transfer of currency. Furthermore, Article 14 provides that in order to be eligible, investment must be made into a developing country.

21 World Bank Group, "Guidelines on the Treatment of Foreign Direct Investment" (1992) *Legal Framework for the Treatment of Foreign Investment: Volume II: Guidelines* (1992) 35–44.

22 See Ibrahim F.I. Shihata, "The Multilateral Investment Guarantee Agency" (1986) 20 *International Lawyer* 485, See also Article 2(a) of the Convention Establishing the Multilateral Investment Guarantee Agency, 1985.

23 See Article 2 of the Convention Establishing the Multilateral Investment Guarantee Agency.

In addition to this, the World Bank also encouraged potential host States to create environments that would attract foreign direct investment. For many resource-rich nations, this entailed liberalizing their economies and revising their investment codes.[24] Host States thus began introducing preferential tax regimes and addressing issues related to compensation for expropriated property. In addition to this, they also included provisions related to the externalization of profits and the settlement of disputes by arbitration. States needed to implement such legislation in order to secure financial assistance from international financial institutions.[25]

1.4 The relationship between foreign investors and host States

The relationship between the host State and the foreign investor is characterized by a long-term business relationship. This typically entails entering into long-term agreements, under which the investor is to provide much needed capital in order to explore and exploit the natural resources of the host State. The host State on the other hand will obtain royalties and other forms of taxation from the investor. The aim of this section is to look at the perspectives of both parties and their expectations in such long-term relationships.

Mineral-rich nations typically lack the finance or technical know-how needed to explore and exploit their vast mineral reserves. Because of this, they will typically seek to attract foreign direct investment, which brings in the much-needed capital. In attracting such investment, host States will offer all sorts of incentives, such as tax breaks and other kinds of benefits. These are intended to improve the investor's ease of doing business in the host State and increase their prospect of making a profit.

Foreign investment certainly does have some positive impact on the economy of the host State. Not only does it provide capital, it also creates jobs. In addition to this, it also brings indirect growth to other sectors of the economy. In principle, therefore, foreign direct investment brings with it a lot of benefits to the host State.[26]

The investor's main intention when entering into these concession agreements is to make a profit. However, such prospects may be diminished by the non-commercial risks associated with long-term foreign investments. These included the risk of nationalization or premature termination of the concession agreement. These particularly manifest in the advanced stages of the resource nationalism cycle, which is when States seek to maximize the benefits of their natural

24 Sangwani Patrick Ng'ambi, *Resource Nationalism in International Investment Law* (Routledge 2016).

25 Sornarajah (n 1) 24.

26 James C. Baker, *Foreign Direct Investment in Less Developed Countries: The Role of ICSID and MIGA* (Quorum Books 1999) 5.

resources.[27] Foreign investors rely heavily on financial institutions to give them capital for their projects. Therefore, it is imperative that these non-commercial risks are ameliorated. Without this, financiers would be reluctant to release the capital needed for the project.

This is further compounded by the fact that the State often offers certain incentives when the price of the natural resource is relatively low. In such instances the State is in a relatively weaker position than the investor and is therefore more willing to acquiesce in the latter's demands.[28] This is further exacerbated in instances where the investor has a plethora of investment options to consider. Once the investment is sunk, however, the State is in a stronger position than the investor. Thus, all promises rendered to the investor are subject to later changes.[29] This is what is referred to as the obsolescing bargaining model.

For this reason, the investor wishes to ensure that it has certain protections at their disposal contractually, legislatively and internationally. On a contractual level, investors rely on certain guarantees such as stabilization clauses.[30] Such clauses are meant to ensure that the host State will not unilaterally terminate the concession using the administrative and legislative prerogatives at their disposal.[31] To ensure that they have recourse to justice outside the fray of the national mechanisms of the host State, investors also insist on arbitration clauses, ensure that disputes arising out the concession will be settled by arbitration. This can be supplemented by a choice-of-law clause, which ensures that the substantive and procedural law of the dispute are settled by the law of a jurisdiction other than the host State.[32] The combination of the three clauses effectively internationalizes the concession agreement.

Investors may also derive their protections from the national law of the host State. Most investment codes, for example, have inserted a plethora of protections for investors through their national legislation. This, for example, includes adopting a compensation standard similar to the "Hull Principle".[33] There are also tax incentives and provisions dealing with the externalization of profits by

27 See generally Thomas W. Wälde, "Renegotiating Acquired Rights in the Oil and Gas Industries: Industry and Political Cycles Meet the Rule of Law" (2008) 1 *Journal of World Energy Law and Business* 55.

28 Erik J. Woodhouse, "The Obsolescing Bargain Redux? Foreign Investment in the Electric Power Sector in Developing Countries" (2006) 38 *New York University Journal of International Law and Politics* 121, 130.

29 See generally Raymond Vernon, *Sovereignty at Bay: The Multinational Spread of US Enterprises* (Longman 1971).

30 Joseph Nna Emeka, "Anchoring Stabilization Clauses in International Petroleum Contracts" (2008) 42 *International Lawyer* 1317, 1319.

31 Christopher T. Curtis, "The Legal Security of Economic Development Agreements" (1988) 29 *Harvard International Law Journal* 317, 346.

32 Dolzer and Schreuer (n 2) 81.

33 See, for example, Section 19(2) of the Zambian Development Agency Act which provides that "Any compensation payable under this section shall be made promptly at market value and shall be fully transferable at the applicable exchange rate in the currency in which the investment was originally made, without deductions for taxes, levies and other duties, except where those are due".

the host State. Moreover, investors can also rely on the protections afforded to them through BITs, Multilateral Trade Agreements and Regional Investment Agreements. Examples of the latter two include the Energy Charter Treaty (ECT), North American Free Trade Area (NAFTA) and the Southern African Development Community (SADC) Protocol on Finance and Investment.

They can also rely on investment insurance. Thus, public institutions such as MIGA are certainly at their disposal. In addition, American owned companies can rely on the Overseas Private Investment Corporation (OPIC) which operates under the auspices of the US government.[34] The OPIC "helps U.S. businesses invest overseas, fosters economic development in new and emerging markets, complements the private sector in managing risks associated with foreign direct investment, and supports U.S. foreign policy".[35] Also available are private institutions such as the Lloyds of London and the American Insurance Group (AIG).

1.5 An overview of investment arbitration

Of concern to the investor is whether any arising dispute between them and the host State will be heard by an impartial tribunal.[36] Having their dispute heard by the national court, for example, is not a very attractive option to the investor because may give the host State an unfair advantage. This is particularly the case in developing countries, where the national courts are not seen as fully independent from the host State. In such circumstances, the national courts may render a decision in favour of the host State, even in instances where the evidence really does not support such a decision. To address this issue, investors insist on the insertion of arbitration clauses in their concession agreements.

Arbitration is the process through which disputes are heard, either by an individual or panel of individuals called an arbitral tribunal. The tribunal derive their authority from the arbitration clause. Thus, in order to have recourse to arbitration in an investment dispute, there must be a written agreement to arbitrate. This could, for example, be accomplished through an arbitration clause in a concession agreement, through national legislation or through a BIT.

The first advantage of having an arbitration clause in a concession agreement is that the national courts must respect and uphold valid arbitration clauses. This is provided for in Article II(3) of the Convention on the Recognition and Enforcement of Foreign Arbitral Awards (the New York Convention). It provides that, "The court of a Contracting State, when seized of an action in a matter in respect of which the parties have made an agreement within the meaning of this article, shall, at the request of one of the parties, refer the parties to arbitration, unless it finds the said agreement is null and void, inoperative[,] or incapable of being performed".

34 Ashton B. Inniss, "Rethinking Political Risk Insurance: Incentives for Investor Risk Mitigation" (2010) 16 *Southwestern Journal of International Law* 477, 488.

35 Ibid.

36 Sornarajah (n 1) 286.

The second advantage is that any decision rendered by an arbitral tribunal is that it is binding and enforceable. The process of seeking recognition and enforcement is fostered through the New York Convention.[37] Furthermore, decisions rendered the International Centre for Settlement of Investment Disputes (ICSID) have a special status under international law. This is seen in Article 54(1) of the ICSID Convention which provides that any award rendered by the ICSID Tribunal is binding and has the same binding force of a judgment at national level. Thus, refusal to directly apply an award rendered by the ICSID Tribunal is a breach of international law.

The other advantage of having a matter decided by arbitration is that the laws relating to international arbitration provide for protections against the unilateral termination of the contract by the host State. The principle of separability is one such protection. Under this principle, an arbitration clause embedded in a contract is seen as separate from the parent contract. Thus, even if the main contract elapses or is avoided, the arbitration clause continues to subsist. A State, therefore, cannot absolve its responsibility to appear before an arbitral tribunal by simply cancelling the contract. Thus, in the case of *LIAMCO v Libya*,[38] Mahmassani said:

> It is widely accepted in international law and practice that an arbitration clause survives the unilateral termination by that State of the contract in which it is inserted and continues to be in force even after that termination. This is a logical consequence of the interpretation of the intention of the contracting parties, and appears to be one of the basic conditions for creating a favourable climate of foreign investment.[39]

A further advantage of arbitration is the principle of *kompetenz-kompetenz*. Under this principle, the arbitral tribunal has the ability to decide on its own competence or jurisdiction over the matter before them.[40] This principle is found in Article 16(1) of the United Nations Commission on International Trade Law (UNCITRAL) Model Law on International Commercial Arbitration which states that, "the arbitral tribunal may rule on its own jurisdiction, including any objections with respect to the existence or validity of the arbitration agreement". It is also found in Article 41(1) of the ICSID Convention, which states that "The Tribunal shall be the judge of its own competence". The advantage with this is that it prevents lawyers from challenging the competence of arbitrators, as a means of stalling the process of arbitration, by averting early judicial interference with the process of arbitration.[41]

37 http://www.uncitral.org/uncitral/en/uncitral_texts/arbitration/NYConvention.html

38 *Libyan American Oil Company (LIAMCO) v Libya* (1981) 20 ILM 1.

39 Ibid 40.

40 George A. Bermann, "The 'Gateway' Problem in International Commercial Arbitration" (2012) 37 *Yale Journal of International Law* 1, 14–15.

41 Ashley Cook, "Kompetenz-Kompetenz: Varying Approaches and a Proposal for a Limited Form of Kompetenz-Kompetenz" (2014) *Pepperdine Law Review* 17, 19.

Since the early 1990s there has been a dramatic rise in the number of investment law related case law.[42] This has been the case because of the growing number of BITs, which have made arbitration available as a recourse to justice for injured investors. However, a few disadvantages arise as a result of this dramatic increase.

The first disadvantage is the divergence of arbitral awards. This is owing to the fact that the composition of arbitral tribunals varies. As a result, the thinking will vary and as such the decisions of such tribunals will not always be the same. This has led to concerns about consistency and coherence in the body of case law relating to international investment law.[43]

The second disadvantage is that States often find themselves in the role of respondents, in arbitral cases.[44] States are constantly having to defend themselves against claims by foreign investors. This has proven burdensome. In addition to this, international investment law and investment arbitration restrict States to perform their legitimate public functions. One of these functions is the right to regulate.[45] As such, the current system of international investment law and international arbitration is not without its difficulties.

1.6 The issue of gender and human rights in the context of international investment law

Foreign direct investment is often fostered by some kind of contractual relationship between the investor and the host State. In a resource-rich nations, this contractual relationship is governed by concession agreements, which could span for a period of thirty years or more.[46]

Given the substantial resources that investors pour into the host State, it is in the investor's pecuniary interest to ensure that the concession or development agreement subsists for the period stipulated. However, given the long-term nature of such agreements, they will invariably be subjects to a plethora of non-commercial risks. There are myriad ways in which investments can be protected. This includes insurance schemes, such as the *MIGA*, which operates under the auspices of the World Bank.[47] In addition to this, investors insist on the insertion of contractual undertakings from the host State which are designed to protect their investment. These will come in the form of stabilization clauses.

42 Dolzer and Schreuer (n 2) 11.

43 See Rudolf Dolzer, "Perspectives for Investment Arbitration: Consistency as a Policy Goal?" (2012) 3 *Transnational Dispute Management* 3

44 Dolzer and Schreuer (n 2) 11.

45 See, for example, Lorenzo Cotula, "Reconciling Regulatory Stability and Evolution of Environmental Standards in Investment Contracts: Towards a Rethink of Stabilization Clauses" (2008) 1 *Journal of World Energy Law & Business* 158.

46 Dolzer and Schreuer (n 2) 21.

47 See Ibrahim F.I. Shihata, "The Multilateral Investment Guarantee Agency" (1986) 20 *International Lawyer* 485–497. See also Article 2(a) of the Convention Establishing the Multilateral Investment Guarantee Agency, 1985.

Stabilization clauses essentially freeze or limit the laws that are applicable to certain projects. The host State under the clauses essentially undertakes not to take any legislative or administrative actions that will adversely affect the investor's interests.

Given the fact that such clauses freeze the law for as long as the contract subsists there has been debate on the negative impact stabilization clauses have on the progressive development of human rights in the host State. There has been some debate on the impact that these clauses essentially freezing the law will have on the development of new human rights laws.[48] The aim of this research is to take this debate further and look at the impact of these clauses on the development of gender laws in resource rich nations. It will particularly look at the compatibility of the Gender Equity and Equality Act, 2015 and the Employment Code Act, No. 3 of 2019.

The main issue here is that the investor is exposed to various risks when they commence with operations in the host State. These risks are particularly evident in the advanced stages of the resource nationalism cycle.[49] This cycle begins when the host State grants a concession to the investor, who is invariably a foreign company, because it lacks sufficient capital or know-how needed to exploit their vast endowments of natural resources. The cycle ends with the host government wishing to exert greater control over its natural resources, once the operations have commenced and have become more profitable. This could either lead to raised taxes or outright nationalization of the investor's assets.

Wary of such eventualities, foreign investors often insist on the insertion of inter alia, stabilization clauses.[50] These are provisions that generally state that, for a given period of time, the government is precluded from making any legislative changes or taking administrative action that will have an adverse effect on the rights contained within the concession agreement. Therefore, in an instance where there is a conflict between the contractual rights contained within the concession containing a stabilization clause and subsequent municipal law, the former will always take precedence.[51] Although arbitral tribunals, for practical

48 See Lorenzo Cotula, "Regulatory Takings, Stabilization Clauses and Sustainable Development" (2008) Global Forum on International Investment, https://www.oecd.org/investment/globalforum/40311122.pdf, Prem Sikka, "Accounting for Human Rights: The Challenge of Globalization and Foreign Investment Agreements" (2011) 22 *Critical Perspectives on Accounting* 811, Jernej L. Cernic, "Corporate Human Rights Obligations under Stabilization Clauses" (2010) 11 *German Law Journal* 210.

49 See generally Thomas W. Wälde, "Renegotiating Acquired Rights in the Oil and Gas Industries: Industry and Political Cycles Meet the Rule of Law" (2008) 1 *Journal of World Energy Law and Business* 55.

50 Piero Bernardini, "Investment Protection under Bilateral Investment Treaties and Investment Contracts" (2001) 2 *Journal of World Investment* 235, 241.

51 See *Sapphire International Petroleum Ltd. v. National Iranian Oil Co. (NIOC)* (1967) 35 I.L.R. 136, *Saudi Arabia v. Arabian American Oil Co. (Aramco)* (1963) 27 I.L.R. 117, *BP v Libya* (1979) 53 I.L.R. 297 and *Texaco Overseas Oil Petroleum Co./California Asiatic Oil Co. v Libya* (1978) 17 ILM 1.

reasons, do not claim the right to compel specific performance, their respect for stabilization clauses and the sanctity of contracts is reflected in the compensation awards they render.[52]

It can be seen that stabilization clauses are drafted in a way that insulates the investor from the obligation of implementing new laws.[53] The difficulty with such a position is that it leads to rigidity in the contracts. This is owing to the fact that the host State is prohibited from passing new laws that have an adverse effect on the investor. New obligations under that develop from gender laws passed subsequently to the signing of concession agreements may thus be deemed incompatible with the stabilization clauses contained in concession agreements. In essence, therefore, stabilization clauses may potentially be a veto on development of gender law in resource-rich nations.

The focus of this research will be the natural resource sector. Most of the case law covered in this study deals with the oil and petroleum industry. The case study on Zambia will deal with copper mining concessions in Zambia and how the stabilization clauses contained therein may have an adverse impact on the development of gender laws in Zambia. In addition, this study deals exclusively with foreign investment as opposed to domestic investment. This distinction is made because although foreign investment is governed by some domestic legislation, it is largely governed by international investment law. Therefore, the rights and obligations are of an international character. These rights and obligations will be reflected in the cases covered in this thesis.

The geographical and chronological scope of the case study in this thesis is generally limited to the Republic of Zambia. However, it will make occasional reference to other jurisdictions. This research is important as the development of gender laws inevitably benefits 50% of the population living in resource-rich nations.

This research is therefore significant because it examines the effect of stabilization clauses on the development of gender law, by carefully scrutinizing the cases and scholarly writings that exist on the subject. In turn, my research will benefit not only Zambia but any other resource-rich country.

1.7 Outline of the chapters

This chapter has given a general overview of the evolution the international standards relating to investment protection. It showed that the need for an international minimum standard was not seen as necessary prior to 1945 because investment existed in the context of colonialism. Because the legal systems of the

52 See Jason W. Yackee, "*Pacta Sunt Servanda* and State Promises to Foreign Investors before Bilateral Investment Treaties: Myth and Reality" (2009) 32 *Fordham International Law Journal* 1550.

53 Andrea Schlemberg, "Stabilization Clauses Human Rights: A Research Project Conducted for the IFC and the UN Special Representative to the Secretary General on Business and Human Rights" (United Nations 2008) 4.

colonial powers and their colonies were integrated, any investment protections needed were provided by the former. This changed between 1945 and 1990 which saw the dissolution of most empires and the emergence of independent States who asserted the need for both political and economic independence. The latter entailed greater control over natural resources, which led to the emergence of the principle of permanent sovereignty over natural resources, which espoused that States could do whatsoever they wished with natural resources found within their jurisdiction. This principle was the basis upon which many host States nationalized assets belonging to foreign investors and putting them under the control of the State. By 1990 however, economic decline prompted host States to encourage the flow of foreign investment. This was ensured through investment protections through BITs. This chapter also gave an introduction to the issue of stabilization clauses and how they may hinder host States from passing new gender equality laws.

Chapter 2 of this book will discuss the doctrine of permanent sovereignty over natural resources. It will be seen that this doctrine espouses that host States have the right to do whatsoever they wish with minerals found within their jurisdiction. This doctrine emerged after the Second World War, when mineral-rich nations wished to acquire both political and economic independence. In order to acquire the latter, mineral-rich nations sought to exert more authority over their natural resources. Hence the introduction of the principle of permanent sovereignty over natural resources. A plethora of rights arise out of this doctrine, although this book focusses mainly on: (1) The right to freely dispose of natural resources, (2) The right to explore and exploit natural resources freely, (3) The right to use natural resources for development and (4) The right to regulate foreign investment. It will also focus on the following duties: (1) the duty to exercise permanent sovereignty over natural resources for the purposes of national development, (2) the duty to respect the rights of indigenous groups, (3) the duty to treat investors in accordance with international law and (4) the duty to compensate the investor in the event that the State unilaterally terminates a concession agreement.

Discussion of the doctrine of permanent sovereignty over natural resources in this book is important, because it is the basis upon which States enter into concession agreements with foreign investors. Moreover, this is the principle that is frequently invoked when host States choose to unilaterally abrogate contracts with foreign investors, using their administrative and legislative prerogatives. It is for this reason that investors often insist on certain protections, which is the topic of discussion in Chapter 3.

Chapter 3 examines political risk and the ways in which investors choose to protect themselves, especially through stabilization clauses. The chapter highlights that it is a major concern of the investor that the contract subsists for the duration stipulated within the concession agreement. This is owing to the fact that the host State retains certain prerogatives that it can utilize to override the contractual interests contained in the concession agreement. In order to avert this, investors will insist on the insert of stabilization clauses in the concession agreement.

Stabilization clauses represent a promise from the host State that it will not use its administrative or legislative prerogatives in a manner that has a material adverse effect on the investment. The effect of this clause is to freeze the law of the host State or at least ensure that no provision in the concession agreement can be overridden without the express consent of the investor. In this sense, they act as a buffer against the advanced stages of the resource nationalism cycle. In the advanced stages of this cycle, host States seek to exercise greater control over their natural resources. This can either be accomplished through taxation or outright nationalization of assets belonging to the investor.

It will be clear from the case law examined in this book that these clauses are respected and upheld by arbitral tribunals. As such, breach of contracts containing stabilization clauses will elicit payment of compensation. The prospect of paying such compensation, whilst protecting the legitimate expectations of the investor may deter host States from developing new human rights, which will be the topic of discussion in Chapter 4.

Chapter 4 will discuss stabilization clauses and human rights. It will be seen in this book that the aim of stabilization clauses is to insulate investors from non-commercial risks associated with foreign direct investment. In the event that the State unilaterally abrogates a concession agreement, it generally becomes liable to compensate the investor. When determining the amount payable the arbitral tribunals take into account the legitimate expectations of the investor during the timeframe that the contract was meant to subsist.

The duty to compensate is unquestionable. What is not clear is which standard of compensation is applicable under international investment law. This is because there are two standards of compensation under international investment law: the Hull Principle and the appropriate compensation standard. It will be established in this book, however, that regardless of standard adopted, lost future profits are typically considered when rendering the compensation award.

Chapter 4 will then discuss the human rights concerns that arise from the rigid application of stabilization clauses. It will be seen that stabilization clauses are certainly a source of liability for host States who wish to develop and implement new human rights legislation. This particularly arises when compliance with new human rights obligations adds to the operating expenses of the foreign investor. In such a case, the State would have to compensate the investor for these additional costs.

For developing countries, like the Republic of Zambia, this may have far-reaching consequences for the development of human rights. This is because any new laws will inevitably increase the obligations of mining companies operating in Zambia. The monetary consequences associated with improving human rights law may act as a deterrent to developing countries developing these laws. This is also applicable to gender equity and equality laws, which is the topic of Chapter 5 of this book.

Chapter 5 will discuss the effect of stabilization clauses on the government's ability to pass new gender equality laws. Chapter 5 consists of a case study of the Republic of Zambia which relies quite heavily on its mining industry. It will be seen that the process of fostering foreign direct investment into the Republic of Zambia is accomplished through development agreements. Under these agreements are tax incentives. To ensure that these incentives subsist for the timeframe envisaged, there are stabilization clauses and tax stability clauses inserted therein. This ensures that the government does not use its prerogatives to pass measures that have a material adverse effect on the rights contained therein.

The difficulty is that the government has passed various pieces of legislation since entering into these development agreements. Although these have enhanced gender equity and equality in the Republic of Zambia, they may also increase the operation costs of mining companies. This could potentially lead to the initiation of arbitral proceedings against the government of Zambia, who may then have to compensate the investor.

2 The doctrine of permanent sovereignty over natural resources

2.1 Introduction

The end of the Second World War saw the dissolution of many colonial empires. Previously subjugated nations thus became independent and sovereign States.[1] Many of these nations were well endowed in natural resources. As a facet of sovereignty and self-determination, these resource rich nations demanded the right to exploit their natural resources for the purposes of economic development and to better their prospects of economic growth.[2] To attain this goal resource-rich nations saw the need to assert themselves on issues such as the control of their natural resources which were in the hands of foreign companies.[3] It was felt that, this state of affairs made nonsense of their newly acquired sovereignty and undermined their desire to develop and exploit their natural resources.[4]

Within the parameters of this goal was the need to reconsider the concession agreements formalized prior to their independence, a plethora of which were perceived as "inequitable and onerous".[5] This was certainly the case in *Aminoil v Kuwait*,[6] where the concession was granted to Aminoil before Kuwait had obtained her independence from Great Britain. This, of course, was by no means an isolated case. The need of developing countries to assert authority over

1 Adeoye Akinsanya, "Permanent Sovereignty over Natural Resources and the Future of Foreign Investment" (1978) 7 *Journal of International Studies* 124, 126.

2 Lilian A. Miranda, "The Role of International Law in Intrastate Natural Resource Allocation: Sovereignty, Human Rights, and People-Based Development" (2012) 45 *Vanderbilt Journal of Transnational Law* 785, 794, Andreas R. Ziegler and Louis-Philippe Gratton, "Investment Insurance" in Peter Muchlinski, Federico Ortino and Christoph Schreuer (eds), *The Oxford Handbook of International Investment Law* (OUP 2008) 526.

3 Samuel K.B. Asante, "Restructuring Transnational Mineral Agreements" (1979) 73 *American Journal of International Law* 335, 340.

4 Ibid.

5 Subrata Roy Chowdhury, "Permanent Sovereignty over Natural Resources: Substratum of the Seoul Declaration" in Paul de Wart, Paul Peters and Erik Denters (eds), *International Law and Development* (Martinus Nijhoff 1988) 61.

6 (1982) 21 I.L.M. 976.

natural resources led to the birth of the international law principle of permanent sovereignty over natural resources.[7]

The principle of permanent sovereignty over natural resources evolved through various United Nations General Assembly Resolutions.[8] However, arguably the "landmark resolution" was the United Nations General Assembly Resolution 1803 (XVII).[9] The evolution of the principle eventually culminated in the Charter of Economic Rights and Duties of States (CERDS) which as the name suggests highlights the rights and duties of States. The next section of this chapter will discuss the general evolution of the principle of permanent sovereignty over natural resources. Section 2.3 will then look at the rights under the principle of permanent sovereignty over natural resources. Section 2.4 will then discuss the duties of States under the principle. Finally, Section 2.5 will consist of a conclusion.

2.2 The doctrine of permanent sovereignty over natural resources

2.2.1 Evolution of the doctrine

The principle of permanent sovereignty over natural resources essentially dictates that resource-rich nations should have control over their natural resources. However, that control is contingent upon the State utilizing the resources for national development. In addition, in exercising the rights attached to this principle the State must act within the parameters of international law. The principle of permanent sovereignty over natural resources was developed over four phases.[10] The first phase took place between 1952 until the adoption of resolution 1803 (XVII) in 1962. The second phase took place between 1962 and 1973 where "the landmark resolution 1803 (XVII) was adopted, reiterated and reaffirmed in a number of other resolutions".[11] The third phase occurred during the Sixth Special Session in May 1974 which eventually led to the adoption of the Charter on 12 December 1974. The fourth phase essentially occurs in the aftermath of 1974 – subsequently to the adoption of the Charter. Implicitly the fourth phase is still in a state of evolution.

7 Lila Barrera-Hernándes, "Sovereignty over Natural Resources under Examination: The Inter-American System for Human Rights and Natural Resource Allocation" (2006) 12 *Annual Survey of International and Comparative Law* 43, 45.

8 See General Assembly Resolution 523 (VI) of 12 January 1952, on Integrated Economic Development and Commercial Agreements.

9 Subrata Roy Chowdhury, "Permanent Sovereignty over Natural Resources" in Kamal Hossain and Subrata Roy Chowdhury (eds), *Permanent Sovereignty over Natural Resources in International Law* (Frances Pinter 1984) 2. See also Emeka Duruigbo, "Permanent Sovereignty and Peoples' Ownership of Natural Resources in International Law" (2006) 38 *George Washington International Law Review* 33, 38.

10 Chowdhury Ibid 3–6.

11 Ibid 3.

During the first phase, which occurred between 1952 and 1962, various resolutions had been passed relating to the principle of permanent sovereignty over natural resources. The focus was on the right of mineral-rich countries to utilize their natural resources as part of their sovereignty, which, in turn, was a facet of self-determination.[12] The first of these was General Assembly Resolution 523 (VI), which recognized the right of under-developed countries "to determine freely the use of their natural resources", with the added proviso that they do this in order to advance the economic development of their nations.[13] The sentiments expressed herein were echoed in the subsequent General Assembly Resolution 626 (VII)[14] which is seen as the genesis of the doctrine of permanent sovereignty over natural resources.[15]

Under General Assembly Resolution 1314 (XIII),[16] it was recognized that the General Assembly needed to be kept fully informed on the doctrine of permanent sovereignty over natural resources. This was owing to the fact that two Covenants drafted by the Human Rights Commission included "permanent sovereignty over their wealth and natural resources" To facilitate this they established a Commission on Permanent Sovereignty comprised of both developed and developing countries which was charged with conducting a "full survey of the status of the permanent sovereignty of people and nations over their natural wealth". They were to pay particular regard to "the rights and duties of States under international law and to the importance of encouraging international co-operation in the economic development of under-developed countries".[17] Surveys conducted by this Commission culminated in the landmark General Assembly Resolution 1803 (XVII).[18] It recognized, "The right of people's and nations to permanent sovereignty over their wealth and resources must be exercised in the interest of their national development and the well-being of the people of the State concerned".

12 Ibid.

13 General Assembly Resolution 523 (VI) of 12 January 1952.

14 General Assembly Resolution 626 (VII) of 21 December 1952. See also James N. Hyde, "Permanent Sovereignty over Natural Wealth and Resources" (1956) 50 *American Society of International Law* 854, 854.

15 See Miranda (n 2) 796; Duruigbo (n 9) 38. See also General Assembly Resolution 837 (IX) of 14 December 1954 and Jason W. Yackee, "*Pacta Sunt Servanda* and State Promises to Foreign Investors before Bilateral Investment Treaties: Myth and Reality" (2009) 32 *Fordham International Law Journal* 1550, 1560.

16 General Assembly Resolution 1314 (XIII) of 12 December 1958.

17 See General Assembly Resolution 1515 (XV) of 15 December 1960 reemphasizing that whilst permanent sovereignty over natural resources had rights attached to it; these did come with duties.

18 General Assembly Resolution 1803 (XVII) of 14 December 1962, See also Marilda Rosado de Sá Ribeiro, "Sovereignty over Natural Resources Investment Law and Expropriation: The Case of Bolivia and Brazil" (2009) 2 *Journal of World Energy Law & Business* 129, 130 and Nico Schrijver, "Natural Resource Management and Sustainable Development" in Thomas G. Weiss and Sam Daws (eds), *The Oxford Handbook on the United Nations* (OUP 2007) 596.

The second phase occurred between 1962 and 1973. This period has generally been described as one characterized by nationalism and States exerting greater control over the exploitation of their natural resources.[19] It comes as no surprise therefore that this period also consisted of a number of resolutions adopting, reaffirming and reiterating resolution 1803 (XVII).[20] In addition, a Working Group on the CERDS was established under Resolution 45 (III)[21] and enlarged under General Assembly Resolution 3037 (XXVII).[22]

The third phase occurred during the Sixth Special Session of the General Assembly which took place on 1 May 1974. This session eventually led to the adoption of the CERDS.[23] There are many rights emanating from this Charter.[24] Article 2(2)(c) quite explicitly postulates that States have the right to "nationalize, expropriate or transfer ownership of foreign property". The condition attached is that the State pays "appropriate compensation" which is to be settled under the auspices of domestic law and domestic tribunals, unless otherwise agreed.

Article 2(1) of the Charter says that the State can freely dispose of its natural resources. It is as a result of this right that States possess the authority to enter into agreements with multinational corporations. It is imperative however, that these agreements are freely entered into.[25] Whilst a State can enter into an agreement, a question that has been intensely debated is whether a State can unilaterally abrogate these agreements.[26] Under the doctrine of permanent sovereignty over natural resources the State also has the right to regulate and supervise foreign investment[27] and the right to nationalize foreign owned property.[28] However, with this right also comes the duty to observe the tenets of international law vis-à-vis the taking of foreign-owned property. This includes the duty to compensate foreign-owned corporations. Furthermore, there is duty to utilize the natural resources in a way that advances economic development.[29]

19 Janeth Warden-Fernandez, "The Permanent Sovereignty over Natural Resources: How It Has Been Accommodated within the Evolving Economy" (2000) *CEPMLP Annual Review Article 4*, 3, http://www.dundee.ac.uk/cepmlp/car/html/car4_art4.htm.

20 Chowdhury (n 9) 3. See, for example, General Assembly Resolution 2158 (XXI) of 25 November 1966, General Assembly Resolution 2386 (XXIII) of 19 December 1968, General Assembly Resolution 2692 (XXV) of 11 December 1970, United Nations Conference on Trade and Development (UNCTAD) Resolution 88 (XII) of 19 October 1972, General Assembly Resolution 3171 (XXVIII) of December 1973.

21 Resolution 45 (III) of the 18th May 1972.

22 General Assembly Resolution 3037 (XXVII) of 19 December 1972, See also General Assembly Resolution 3082 (XXVIII) of 6 December 1973.

23 Resolution 3281 (XXIX).

24 See Schrijver, *Sovereignty over Natural Resources: Balancing Rights and Duties* (CUP 1997) 258–298.

25 *Texaco v Libya* (1978) 17 ILM, paragraphs 66–67.

26 For an overview see Esa Paasirvirta, "Internationalization and Stabilization of Contracts versus State Sovereignty" (1989) 60 *British Yearbook of International Law* 315, 316–323.

27 Article 2(2)(a).

28 Schrijver (n 24) 271–274.

29 Ibid 306–344.

The fourth phase occurs in the aftermath of the adoption of the Charter. The evolution and acceptance of this doctrine is determined by examining treaties that have been concluded since 1974. It has been noted that myriad treaties do reflect the rights and duties espoused in the Charter. However, given the adoption of bilateral investment treaties, which advocate full rather than appropriate compensation, the universal acceptance of the Charter may be questioned.[30]

2.2.2 Legal status of the principle of permanent sovereignty over natural resources

Because the Charter stems from a General Assembly resolution, there are questions as to whether the rights and duties contained therein are binding. On the one hand, it is argued that General Assembly resolutions are not binding.[31] It is recognized that the General Assembly does possess "quasi-legislative" functions.[32] However, it is difficult to argue that the General Assembly is a legislative organ.[33] This is first owing to the fact that there is an objection to two-thirds majority binding the minority. Second, to bind States under General Assembly resolutions may circumvent the traditional treaty making process which, under some national constitutions, requires ratification in order for the State to be bound.[34]

On the other hand, to completely disregard the principles espoused in these General Assembly resolutions would be erroneous. Because of the general procedures that lead to the eventual vote and adoption of a resolution, it could be argued that they constitute evidence of customary international law.[35] A customary rule "comes into existence only where there are acts of State in conformity with it, coupled with the belief that those acts are required by international law".[36] These resolutions become customary norms on the basis that the General Assembly is itself a vehicle through which the States form and express the practice of international law are manifested.[37] The resolution is drafted in such a way that it can win the support of the majority of the Assembly. Typically, more

30 Chowdhury (n 9) 5–6 and Schrijver (n 24) 258–298.

31 See generally James Crawford, *The Creation of States in International Law* (2nd edn, OUP 2006) 113, Alan Boyle and Christine Chinkin, *The Making of International Law* (OUP 2007) 116 and Gregory J. Kerwin, "The Role of United Nations General Assembly Resolutions in Determining Principles of International Law in United States Courts" (1983) 4 *Duke Law Journal* 876.

32 Philippe Sands and Pierre Klein, *Bowett's Law of International Institutions* (6th edn, Sweet & Maxwell 2009) 28.

33 Ibid.

34 Ibid.

35 Ibid 27–28.

36 Samuel A. Bleicher, "The Legal Significance of Re-Citation of General Assembly Resolutions" (1969) 63 *American Journal of International Law* 444, 449.

37 Muthucumaraswamy. Sornarajah, *The International Law on Foreign Investment* (3rd edn, CUP 2010) 446.

than a bare majority must be ensured before a vote will be called.[38] The resolution will often represent a harmonization of the conflicting views that might have been expressed, prior to the vote being called.[39] Therefore, by the time it is being adopted, it is an expression of the general consensus, which, in turn, can be construed as the formulation of a customary norm.[40]

This book supports the latter view. Arguably, the General Assembly resolutions pertaining to permanent sovereignty over natural resources do form a part of customary law. This view has been supported by various arbitral tribunals. For example, in the case of *LIAMCO v Libya*,[41] the arbitrator held that "the said Resolutions, if not a unanimous source of law, are evidence of the recent dominant trend of international opinion concerning the sovereign right of States over natural resources".[42] This clearly shows that even arbitral tribunals recognize the general resolutions on permanent sovereignty over natural resources, as evidence of customary law.

This position was also reflected in *Texaco v Libya*.[43] Here the arbitral tribunal took the view that Resolution 1803 reflected the tenets of customary international law.[44] They arrived at this conclusion on the basis that the said resolution referred to international law when it spoke of nationalization.[45] Moreover, the aforementioned resolution had received the universal assent of both developed and developing countries.[46] They further opined that General Assembly Resolution 1803 ought to be contrasted with the CERDS, which, in the arbitrators view, "must be analyzed as a political rather than as a legal declaration concerned with the ideological strategy of development and, as such, supported only by non-industrialized States".[47]

Furthermore, it could be argued that the resolutions pertaining to permanent sovereignty over natural resources are a reflection of rights and duties that already existed under international law.[48] For example, it was already

38 Bleicher (n 36) 451.
39 Ibid.
40 Ibid.
41 (1977) 62 ILR 141.
42 Ibid paragraph 100.
43 *Texaco v Libya* (n 25).
44 Ibid 30.
45 Ibid 29. See also Stephen M. Schwebel, "The Story of the U.N.'s Declaration on Permanent Sovereignty over Natural Resources" (1963) 49 *American Bar Association Journal* 463, 469.
46 Ibid.
47 Ibid 30. See also Andreas Lowenfeld, "Investment Agreements and International Law" (2003) 42 *Columbia Journal of Transnational Law* 123, 124 and Eduardo Jiménez de Aréchaga, "Application of the Rules of States Responsibility to the Nationalization of Foreign-Owned Property" in Kamal Hossain (ed), *Legal Aspects of the New International Economic Order* (Frances Pinter 1980) 225.
48 Karol N. Gess, "Permanent Sovereignty over Natural Resources: An Analytical Review of the United Nations Declaration and Its Genesis" (1964) 13 *International and Comparative Law Quarterly*, 398, 411 and Richard R. Baxter, "International Law in 'Her Infinite Variety'" (1980) 29 *International and Comparative Law Quarterly* 549, 564.

generally recognized that the State had the right to nationalize.[49] Once the State nationalized they also had an obligation to pay compensation.[50] This is therefore another reason why it could be argued that the resolutions pertaining to permanent sovereignty over natural resources are generally binding.

In addition, the principle of permanent sovereignty over natural resources has been accepted by the International Court of Justice. This position was reflected in the *East Timor Case.*[51] In more recent times, the principle of permanent sovereignty over natural resources has gained more recognition. In *Congo v Uganda*,[52] the International Court of Justice recognized permanent sovereignty over natural resources as "a principle of customary international law".[53] Given the fact that decisions of the International Court of Justice are a source of international law, it could thus be asserted that the principle of permanent sovereignty over natural resources is a legitimate one and so are the rights and duties emanating therefrom.

It could thus be argued that the principle of permanent sovereignty over natural resources is firmly accepted under international law.[54] It is under this principle that States are able to enter into concession agreements with investors. It is argued that under this principle, the word "permanent" entails that the State has the right to exit these agreements at any given time, regardless of an agreement not to do so.[55] It might appear, therefore, that there is a clash between this principle and the insertion of stabilization clauses in concession agreements.

49 Schrijver (n 24) 271–274.

50 Ibid.

51 *East Timor (Portugal v Australia)* 1995 ICJ 90. See the dissenting opinions of Weeramantry J. at 204 and Skubiszeweski J. at 264.

52 *Case Concerning Armed Activities on the Territory of the Congo (Democratic Republic of the Congo v Uganda)* I.C.J. Reports 2005, p. 168.

53 Paragraph 244. Note however that it does not apply in situations of "looting, pillage and exploitation of certain natural resources by members of the army of a State militarily intervening in another State". Judge Koroma in his declaration contends that the ICJ's acknowledgement of the principle as a customary norm implies that the rights and duties emanating from it, "remain in effect at all times, including ***during armed conflict and occupation***" (paragraph 11). This can be contrasted with ad hoc Judge Kateka who said that, "The PSNR was adopted in the era of decolonization and the assertion of the rights of newly independent States. It thus would be inappropriate to invoke this concept in a case involving two African countries. This remark is made without prejudice to the right of States to own and or dispose of their natural resources as they wish" (paragraph 56).

54 Robert Dufrense, "The Opacity of Oil: Oil Corporations, Internal Violence, and International Law" (2004) 36 *New York University Journal of International Law and Politics* 331, 354, Chowdhury (n 9) 1, Kamal Hossain, "Introduction" in Kamal Hossain and Subrata Roy Chowdhury (eds). *Permanent Sovereignty over Natural Resources* (Frances Printer 1984) ix–xx, ix, Abul F.M. Maniruzzaman, "International Development Law as Applicable Law to Economic Development Agreements: A Prognostic View" (2001) 20 *Wisconsin International Law Journal* 1, 23 and Nico Schrijver, "Natural Resources, Permanent Sovereignty over" (2010) *Max Planck Encyclopedia of Public International Law*, p 8 http://ilmc.univie.ac.at/uploads/media/PSNR_empil.pdf.

55 Eduardo Jiménez de Aréchaga, "State Responsibility for the Nationalization of Foreign Owned Property" (1978) 11 *New York University Journal of Law and Politics* 179, 179–180.

The next section of this chapter will discuss stabilization clauses and the attitudes of courts and international tribunal to the permanent sovereignty argument.

2.3 Rights and duties under the doctrine

There are various rights associated with the doctrine of permanent sovereignty of natural resources. These are: (1) The right to freely dispose of natural resources, (2) the right to explore and exploit natural resources freely, (3) the right to regain effective control and to compensation for damage, (4) the right to use natural resources for national development, (5) the right to manage natural resources pursuant to national environmental policy, (6) the right to an equitable share in benefits of transboundary natural resources, (7) the right to regulate foreign investment, (8) the right to expropriate or nationalize foreign investment and (9) the right to settle disputes on the basis of national law. Since this book is primarily concerned with concession agreements, its main focus will be on: (1) The right to freely dispose of natural resources, (2) the right to explore and exploit natural resources freely, (3) the right to use natural resources for development and (4) the right to regulate foreign investment.

2.3.1 The right to freely dispose of natural resources

One of the rights emanating from the doctrine of permanent sovereignty over natural resources is the right of a State to freely dispose of the natural resources within its jurisdiction.[56] This in broad terms gives the State the right to do whatsoever it wishes with natural resources, found within its jurisdiction. The right to freely dispose of natural resources is one that is recognized by a number of treaties and covenants. It is also recognized in a number of arbitral awards and judicial decisions. An example of recognition under international treaties and covenants is Article 1(2) of the International Covenant on Civil and Political Rights. It provides that all people may "freely dispose of their natural wealth and resources". This right is also recognized in Article 21(1) of the African Charter on Human and Peoples' Rights. This provision is couched in similar terms to the International Covenant on Civil and Political Rights, in that it recognizes that all people have the right to freely dispose of their natural resources. This is provided that this right is exercised in the "exclusive interest of the people".

Further support for the States right to freely dispose of its natural resources is found in the wording of the preamble of the Biodiversity Convention of 1992. It emphasizes States sovereign rights over their own biological resources.[57]

56 Article 1(2) International Covenant on Civil and Political Rights, December 16, 1966, 999 UNTS 171 (1967), Article 5, United Nations General Assembly Resolution 1515 (XV), Article 21 of the African Charter on Human and Peoples' Rights, June 27, 1981, 1520 UNTS 217.

57 See also Article 15(1) of the Biodiversity Convention of 1992 which provides says, "Recognizing the sovereign rights of States over their natural resources, the authority to determine access to genetic resources rests with the national governments ..."

In addition to this, there is Article 18(1) of the Energy Charter Treaty of 1994 which also recognizes, "state sovereignty and sovereign rights over energy resources".[58] Article 18(3) of the Energy Charter Treaty further provides that:

> Each state continues to hold in particular the rights to decide the geographical areas within its Area to be made available for exploration and development of its energy resources, the optimalization of their recovery and the rate at which they may be depleted or otherwise exploited, to specify and enjoy any taxes, royalties or other financial payments payable by virtue of such exploration and exploitation, and to regulate the environmental and safety aspects of such exploration, development and reclamation within its Area, and to participate in such exploration and exploitation, inter alia, through direct participation by the government or through state enterprises.

It can thus be seen that the right to freely exploit natural resources is recognized in a plethora of international treaties and covenants. This right is also found in arbitral awards and judicial decisions. For example, in the case of *Texaco v Libya*, the arbitral tribunal recognized that territorial sovereignty confers an "exclusive competence" on the State to organize its economic structures as it sees fit. They also have the right to introduce any desirable reforms. This is owing to the fact that a constitutionally authorized government has the sovereign right to choose and freely build an economic and social system, within its territory. The tribunal opined that "International law recognizes that a State has this prerogative just as it has the prerogative to determine freely its political regime and its constitutional institutions".[59]

Implicit within the right to freely dispose of natural resources is the authority to enter into concession agreements with foreign investors. Such concession agreements are typically structured in a way that ensures that the investor explores and exploits natural resources belonging to the host State. The former is then to pay royalties and other taxes to the latter. However, such agreements must be freely entered into. This position was certainly emphasized in the case of *Texaco v Libya*, where the arbitrator opined that when a State enters into an international agreement with any party, it exercises its sovereignty. This is provided that such an agreement is not subject to duress and that "the State has freely committed itself through untainted consent".[60]

There is much debate as to the binding nature of concession agreements, given the "permanent" nature of this sovereignty. This will be discussed further in the next chapter. However, on the one hand there is an argument that States never lose their legal capacity to "change the destination or method of exploration of

58 However, note Article 18(2) of the Energy Charter treaty which provides that, the Treaty shall in no way prejudice the rules in Contracting Parties governing the system of property ownership of energy resources".

59 17 ILM (1978), paragraph 59.

60 *Texaco v Libya* (n 25), paragraphs 66–67.

those resources, whatever arrangements have been made for their exploitation".[61] Therefore, the permanent nature of this sovereignty suggests that States are free to unilaterally abrogate their contractual obligations, in order to regain their right to freely dispose of their natural resources.[62]

However, the difficulty with this position is that it fails to distinguish between the "enjoyment" and the "exercise" of sovereignty. There is certainly a distinction and this was clearly highlighted in *Texaco v Libya*, where the arbitrator opined that the "State retains, within the areas which it has reserved authority over the operation conducted by the concession holder and the continuance of the exercise of its sovereignty is manifested, for example, by the various obligations imposed on the contracting party".[63]A similar view was expressed in *Agip v Congo* where the arbitral tribunal stated that:

> These Stabilisation clauses, freely accepted by the Government, do not affect the principle of its sovereign legislative and regulatory powers, since it retains both in relation to those, whether nationals or foreigners, with whom it has not entered into such obligations, and that, in the present case, changes in the legislative and regulatory arrangements stipulated in the agreement simply cannot be invoked against the other contracting party.[64]

Thus, even though a State enters into a contract State sovereignty still remains intact. However, that sovereignty cannot be exercised in a manner that adversely affects an investor to whom the host State has contractual obligations.[65] As such, in the event that the host State wishes to exercise its sovereignty through nationalizing foreign-owned property, then this must be done in accordance with certain conditions, including the payment of compensation.

There is also a contention that host States can unilaterally abrogate agreements, if there is a fundamental change in circumstances.[66] Change of circumstances, or *rebus sic stantibus* is certainly a principle recognized under international law.[67] This principle is certainly found in the Vienna Convention on Treaties. Article 62(1) of the Convention provides a State may withdraw from a treaty where in

61 Jiménez E. de Aréchaga, "International Law in the Past Third of a Century" in *Recueil des Cours* (1978-I) 159: 1–344 (Sijthoff and Noordhoff 1979) 297.

62 See Somendu Kumar Banerjee, "The Concept of Permanent Sovereignty over Natural Resources: An Analysis" (1968) 8 *Indian Journal of International Law* 515.

63 *Texaco v Libya* (n 25), paragraph 77.

64 *Agip v Congo*, pp. 735–736.

65 Georges Abi-Saab, "Progressive Development of the Principles and Norms of International Law Relating to the New International Economic Order" in UN Doc. A/39/504/Add. 1, 23rd October 1973, paragraph 58 who says that, "sovereignty is the rule and can be exercised at any time, that limitations are the exception and cannot be permanent, but limited in scope and time".

66 Subrata Roy Chowdhury, "Permanent Sovereignty over Natural Resources: Substratum of the Seoul Declaration" in Paul de Wart, Paul Peters and Erik Denters (eds), *International Law and Development* (Matinus Nijhoff 1988) 69.

67 See Article 62(1) of the Vienna Convention on Treaties.

the event that there are unforeseen circumstances and that "(a) the existence of those circumstances constituted an essential basis of the consent of the parties to be bound by the treaty; and (b) the effect of the change is radically to transform the extent of the obligations still to be performed under the treaty". In the *Fisheries Jurisdiction Case (United Kingdom v Iceland)*, the International Court of Justice held that a fundamental change of circumstances may, in certain conditions, absolve the State of its obligations under a treaty. The International Court of Justice further stated that:

> This principle, and the conditions and exceptions to which it is subject, have been embodied in Article 62 of the Vienna Convention on the Law of Treaties, which may in many respects be considered as a codification of existing customary law on the subject of the termination of a treaty relationship on account of change of circumstances.[68]

The change of circumstances must radically transform the extent of the obligations still to be performed by the parties. Such a change must increase the burden of the obligations in such a way that it renders the "performance something essentially different from that originally undertaken".[69]

In the area of international investment law, the principle *rebus sic stantibus* was also supported in *AMCO Asia Corporation v Indonesia*[70] where the ICSID Tribunal opined that the State is entitled to withdraw from a contract, "for reasons which would not be invoked by a private contracting entity, and/or to decide and implement the withdrawal by utilizing procedures which are different from those which can and have to be utilized by a private entity". They go

68 (1973) ICJ Reports, p. 19, paragraph 36.

69 Ibid paragraph 43, p. 21. Justice Elias writing extrajudicially also opined that, "The justification for the application of the doctrine of *rebus sic stantibus* in the modern law of treaties is that a treaty may remain in force for a long time and its provisions may place an unnecessary burden on one of the parties as a result of a fundamental change of circumstances without any hope of redress if the other party should prove difficult. The disgruntled State might eventually be driven to take the law into its own hands. In such cases the doctrine could serve a useful purpose by inducing the other party to come to a compromise or, at least, to secure a solution by legal means. At first, under customary international law, the doctrine has been assumed as a condition implied in every 'perpetual' treaty which would destroy it in the event of a fundamental change of circumstances. Today, the implied term is looked upon as only a fiction intended to reconcile the principle of the dissolution of a treaty in consequence of fundamental change of circumstances with the well-established rule, *pacta sunt servanda*. The truth is that, in the majority of cases, the parties would not have given a thought to the possibility of a change of circumstances and that, if they had done so, they would probably have made other provisions for it. It is nevertheless desirable that the theory of an implied term be rejected and the doctrine be formulated as an objective rule according to which, on the grounds of equity and justice, a fundamental change of circumstances might be invoked as a ground for terminating and withdrawing from a treaty. It remains to add that there is no basis for the older view that the doctrine is confined to 'perpetual' treaties or even 'long-term' ones". See Taslim Olawale Elias, *The Modern Law of Treaties* (Oceania 1974) 121–122.

70 (1985) 24 ILM 1022, 1029.

on further to say that the State protects the nation's public interest and welfare. As such, the State possesses the right to alter or even pull out of an agreement if public interest calls for it. This includes the sovereign prerogative to nationalize or expropriate property or indeed contractual rights previously granted by itself. However, this right must be exercised in the public interest.

It can thus be seen that the host State has the right to freely dispose of its natural resources. This right is firmly supported by international treaties and conventions and also in awards by arbitral tribunals. However, this right can be limited when the State freely enters into concession agreements. Although such agreements can technically be terminated at any time, such termination elicits the payment of compensation. One identifiable exception to this rule is if there has been a change in circumstances. However, this is only applied in limited conditions.

2.3.2 *The right to freely explore and exploit natural resources*

Another right emanating from the doctrine of permanent sovereignty over natural resources is the right of the host State to freely explore and exploit its natural resources. This right is certainly recognized by a preponderance of General Assembly resolutions.[71] It is also recognized in a number of treaties.[72] For example, recognition of the right of a State to freely explore and exploit its natural resources is found in the 1982 Convention on the Law of the Sea. Article 56(1)(a) of the aforementioned Convention says that the State can utilize its sovereign rights for the purposes of "exploring and exploiting, conserving and managing" its natural resources. In addition to this, the right of the host State to freely explore and exploit its natural resources is supported by the International Covenant on Economic Social and Cultural Rights. Article 25 of this Covenant thus postulates that people have the inherent right to fully and freely enjoy and utilize their wealth and natural resources. International Covenant on Civil and Political Rights contains a similar provision.[73]

Moreover, the right is also recognized in Article IV of the Treaty for Amazonian Co-operation of 1978. In this provision, contracting States made a declaration that the exclusive "use and utilization" of natural resources found within their jurisdictions was a facet of sovereignty. It has also found support in the International Court of Justice. Thus in the *Fisheries Jurisdiction Case,* the International Court of Justice held that the State could create a twelve-mile fishery zone for the benefit of its people "to the extent of the special dependence of its people upon the fisheries in the seas around its coasts for their livelihood and economic development".[74]

71 See generally Resolutions 626 (VII), 1803 (XVII), 2158 and 3171.

72 Schrijver (n 24) 265.

73 See Article 47 which says that, "Nothing in the present Covenant shall be interpreted as impairing the inherent right of all peoples to enjoy and utilize fully and freely their natural wealth and resources".

74 (1974) ICJ Reports 34, paragraph 79.

The right was also recognized in the case of *Aminoil v Kuwait* where the government of Kuwait had terminated a concession agreement with Aminoil and effectively nationalized its assets. In this case the arbitral tribunal took into account "profound and general transformation in terms of oil concessions that occurred in the Middle East, and later throughout the world".[75] As a consequence of these changes the State had now become "an associate whose interests had become predominant".[76] As a result of this the Kuwaiti government's decision to terminate Aminoil's concession was in itself legal and was regarded as a step in safeguarding the former's national interests.[77]

It can thus be seen that the right to freely explore and exploit natural resources is a facet of the principle of permanent sovereignty over natural resources. In addition to its recognition under general assembly resolutions, it is also recognized by treaties and awards rendered by international arbitral tribunals. There appears to be no international literature casting doubt on this right.[78]

2.3.3 The right to utilize natural resources for national development

The right to utilize natural resources for national development also stems from the doctrine of permanent sovereignty over natural resources. This is a right that appears frequently in General Assembly resolutions of the United Nations. For example, General Assembly Resolution 626 (VII) provides that States have the right to use and exploit their natural resources for the purposes of "their own progress and economic development". General Assembly Resolution 1803 (XVII) also makes reference to use of natural resources "in the interest of … national development and of the well-being of the people of the State concerned". It also provides that economic agreements entered into should be "such as to further" the national development of resource-rich nations and "shall be based upon respect for their sovereignty over their natural wealth and resources".[79]

The right to utilize natural resources for national development is also supported by the Lomé IV Convention of 1989. Article 220(f) of the aforementioned Convention states that one of the objectives of its signatories is to "contribute to optimal and judicious exploration, conservation, processing, transformation and exploitation of the ACP (African, Caribbean, and Pacific Group) States' natural resources in order to enhance the efforts of ACP States to industrialize and to achieve economic diversification".

75 *Aminoil v Kuwait* (n 6) 1023, paragraph 97.
76 Ibid paragraph 99.
77 *Aminoil* (n 6) paragraph 114.
78 Schrijver (n 24) 265.
79 See also Article 7 of the Charter on the Economic Rights and Duties of States which provides that, "each State has the right and the responsibility … fully to mobilize and use its resources in a manner that promotes the economic development of its people".

The position of international jurisprudence on this right is somewhat discordant. On the one hand there is the case of *Aramco v Saudi Arabia*, which does not seem to support it, and on the other hand there is *Aminoil v Kuwait* which does. The brief fact of the *Aramco* case is that there was an agreement between Aramco and the government of Saudi Arabia. This agreement contained a stabilization clause which purportedly precluded the government from taking steps that would compromise Aramco's contractual rights. These rights included the "exclusive right" or Aramco to "carry away and export petroleum". While this agreement subsisted, the government of Saudi Arabia entered into a transportation agreement with Aristotle Onassis. Aramco thus took the government of Saudi Arabia to arbitration claiming that their contractual rights had been unilaterally abrogated. The arbitral tribunal agreed and contended that, "the rights and obligations of the concessionary accompany are in the nature of acquired rights and cannot be modified without the Company's consent".[80]

The decision in *Aramco* can be contrasted with the case of *Aminoil v Kuwait.* This case also involved a concession containing a stabilization clause, except in this case the government of Kuwait had nationalized assets belonging to Aminoil. The tribunal opined:

> This Concession ... became one of the essential instruments in the economic and social progress of a national community in full process of development. This transformation, progressively achieved, took place at first by means of successive levies going to the State, and then through the growing influence of the State in the economic and technical management of the undertaking ... and the regulation of works and investment programmes. The contract of Concession thus changed its character and became one of those contracts in regard to which, in most legal systems, the State, while remaining bound to respect the contractual equilibrium, enjoys special advantages.[81]

Closely linked to development is the right to manage natural resources according to the national environmental policy. This is supported by the Stockholm Declaration of 1972 that States are permitted to utilize their natural resources. Principle 21 thus provides that "pursuant to their own environmental policies" provided that they do not "cause damage to the environment of other States or of areas beyond the limits of national jurisdiction". It is further supported in Article 193 of the UN Convention on the Law of the Sea which states that "States have the sovereign right to exploit their natural resources pursuant to their environmental policies and in accordance with their duty to protect and preserve the marine environment". Permitting the State to manage resources according to its own environmental national environmental policy permits is advantageous to developing countries. This is owing to the fact that it precludes

80 (1963) 27 ILR 117, 168.

81 *Aminoil v Kuwait* (n 6) paragraph 98.

industrialized nations from using environmental considerations "as an excuse for interference in the internal affairs of the developing countries".[82] As a result developing countries are protected from being held to a high standard that might, in turn, halt the process of national development. For this reason, the right to manage resources according to the national environmental policy accentuates the right to utilize natural resources for national development.

Also tied to the right to utilize natural resources for national development is the right of the State to choose its own economic system. This right is provided for in Article 1 of the Charter on the Economic Rights and Duties of States which states that "Every State has the sovereign and inalienable right to choose its economic system as well as it political, social and cultural systems in accordance with the will of its people, without outside interference, coercion or threat in any form whatsoever". This is a right that has been discussed in the determination of compensation payable by the State to a nationalized corporation. Thus, in the case of *Lithgow v United Kingdom*,[83] Counsel for the European Commission contended that:

> [T]he European States would seem to have a more or less coherent view, according to which public international law requires the payment of at least appropriate compensation where foreign property is being taken. As to the practice it is extremely divergent. I am not aware of one single case where, for nationalisation of whole industries, full compensation was paid by the nationalising state to the foreign owners, without special investment treaties being applicable. In most cases of nationalisation, lump-sum agreements were reached clearly below the value of the assets taken. At least for large scale nationalisation, the notion of sovereignty over natural resources and freedom of decision over the economic order may easily come into conflict with a claim of full compensation.

Although the European Court of Human Rights did not go into great detail on this issue they did indicate that they would not question the State's determination of compensation payable unless the decision was "manifestly without reasonable foundation".[84] In other words, the European Court of Human Rights refused to override this right, without a good reason for doing so.

From this subsection it has been seen that the right to utilize natural resources is yet another facet of the principle of permanent sovereignty over natural resources. It is certainly supported by international law treaty and cases. In addition to this, it is linked to two related rights: namely the right to manage according to the national environmental policy and the right of a State to choose its own economic path.

82 Final Documents of the Tenth Conference of Heads of State or Government of Non-Aligned Countries, Jakarta, 1–6 September 1992, p. 37, paragraph 68.

83 *Lithgow v United Kingdom* (1986) 8 EHRR 329.

84 Ibid 373.

2.3.4 The right to regulate foreign investment and the right to nationalize

Two other rights stemming from the doctrine of permanent sovereignty over natural resources are the right States have to regulate foreign direct investment and the right to nationalize. Included under the right to regulate foreign investment is the right to determine what type of investment flows into the country. Also included here is the right to exercise authority over it once it is within the jurisdiction.

With regard to the right to regulate foreign direct investment, Article 2(2)(a) of the Charter on the Economic Rights and Duties of States clearly stipulates that each State has the right to "regulate and exercise authority over foreign investment within its national jurisdiction". Such regulation is to be in accordance with laws and regulations of the host State. Furthermore, regulation of foreign direct investment must also be in conformity with the State's national objectives and priorities. Furthermore, Article 2(2)(b) of the CERDS provides that States have the right "to regulate and supervise the activities of transnational corporations within its national jurisdiction". States can also take measures to ensure that the activities of multinational corporations conform with its economic and social policies.

The right to regulate foreign direct investment has also been seen in International Labour Organization's Seoul Declaration. Section 5.5 of the Seoul Declaration provides that States have the right "to regulate, exercise authority, legislate and impose taxes in respect of natural resources enjoyed and economic activities exercised and wealth held in their own territories by foreign interests".[85] This provision is only subject to the requirements of international law.

The right to regulate and exercise authority over foreign investment is linked closely to the right to nationalize. Nationalization is the taking over of private property by the State.[86] Definitions have been propounded on what actually amounts to taking. For example, in Article 10(3) of the 1961 Draft Convention on State Responsibility by Sohn and Baxter provides that:

a A "taking of property" includes not only an outright taking of property but also any such unreasonable interference, use, enjoyment or disposal of property as to justify an inference that the owner thereof will not be able to use, enjoy or dispose of the property within a reasonable period of time after the inception of such interference.

b A "taking of the use of property" includes not only an outright taking of property but also any unreasonable interference with the use or enjoyment of property for a limited period of time.[87]

85 Seoul Declaration, section 5.5.

86 Sornarajah (n 37) 365.

87 Louis B. Sohn and Richard R. Baxter, "Responsibility of States for Injuries to the Economic Interests of Aliens" (1961) 55 *American Journal of International Law*, 545, 553.

A similar definition of taking was adopted in the case of *Tippets, Abbett, McCarthy, Stratton v TAMS AFFA*[88] where the tribunal stated that taking of property can occur either through interference with the use of property, or the enjoyment of its benefits. This is the case even where legal title to the said property remains unaffected.[89]

> A deprivation or taking of property may occur under international law through interference by a State in the use of that property or with the enjoyment of its benefits, even where legal title to the property is not affected.

We can also have creeping expropriation which may occur when the State "subjects alien property to taxation, regulation, or other action that is confiscatory, or that prevents, unreasonably interferes with, or unduly delays, effective enjoyment of an alien's property or its removal from the State's territory". Sornarajah has noted that the following can amount to creeping expropriation:

1 Forced sales of property; (2) forced sales of shares; (3) indigenization measures; (4) exercising management control over the investment; (5) inducing others to physically take over the property; (6) failure to provide protection when there is interference with the property of the foreign investor; (7) administrative decisions which cancel licences and permits necessary for the foreign business to function within the State; (8) exorbitant taxation; (9) expulsion of the foreign investor contrary to international law; and (10) acts of harassment such as the freezing of bank accounts, promoting of strikes, lockouts and labour shortages.[90]

This list is by no means exhaustive or definitive.[91] What is important is that the State has taken action that directly or indirectly interferes with the investors use and enjoyment of the property. Other government actions that do not necessarily fit in the list above could nonetheless amount to "measures tantamount to expropriation".[92]

Nationalization is as a general rule legal.[93] International case law certainly supports the first view. A case that illustrates this is the *Case Concerning German*

88 (1984) 6 Iran – US CTR 219.
89 Ibid 225.
90 Sornarajah (n 37) 375.
91 Asif Qureshi and Andreas Ziegler, *International Economic Law* (3rd edn, Sweet & Maxwell 2011) 515.
92 *Azinian v Mexico* (November 1, 1999); *Pope & Talbot v Canada* (June 26, 2000 interim award) or *Middle East Cement Shipping and Handling Co. S.A. v Arab Republic of Egypt* (ICSID Case No. ARB/99/6 – April 12, 2002).
93 See Francisco V. Garcia-Amador, *Special Rapporteur's Report* (International Law Commission 1959).

Interests in Upper Silesia[94] where Poland had nationalized a German factory. The Permanent Court held that although the nationalization in this case was ultimately illegal because it was in breach of a treaty, States do have the sovereign right to take over property within its borders.[95] The legality of nationalization is also endorsed in *General Assembly Resolution 1803* (1962)[96] which states that States do have sovereignty over their natural resources and as such States do have the right to take over property within their jurisdiction. As such, they have the right to nationalize, expropriate or requisition property, provided that it is for a public purpose and accompanied by the payment of "appropriate compensation".[97] This position was reaffirmed in *General Assembly Resolution* 3171 (1973)[98] which affirmed that:

> the application of the principle of nationalization carried out by States, as an expression of their sovereignty in order to safeguard their natural resources, implies that each State is entitled to determine the amount of possible compensation and the mode of payment, and that any disputes which might arise should be settled in accordance with the national legislation of each State carrying out such measures;

Furthermore, the right to nationalize was endorsed in the CERDS.[99] It provided that every State has the right to "nationalize, expropriate or transfer ownership of foreign property". However, this is contingent upon the payment of "appropriate compensation" by the State adopting such measures. Such compensation will take into account the relevant laws and regulations of the host State and any other such circumstances that it considers pertinent.

From the foregoing it can be seen that the State has the right to regulate foreign direct investment, and this is inextricably linked to the right to nationalize. The right to nationalize is contingent on it being for a public purpose and on the payment of appropriate compensation to the nationalized entity.

94 (1926–1928) PCIJ Series A, Nos. 7, 9, 17, 19.

95 (1926) Series A, Nos. 7, 22.

96 Permanent Sovereignty over Natural Resources, G.A. res. 1803 (XVII), 17 U.N. GAOR Supp. (No.17) at 15, U.N. Doc. A/5217 (1962).

97 General Assembly Resolution 1803 (1962) thus provides that, "4. Nationalization, expropriation or requisitioning shall be based on grounds or reasons of public utility, security or the national interest which are recognized as overriding purely individual or private interests, both domestic and foreign. In such cases the owner shall be paid appropriate compensation, in accordance with the rules in force in the State taking such measures in the exercise of its sovereignty and in accordance with international law. In any case where the question of compensation gives rise to a controversy, the national jurisdiction of the State taking such measures shall be exhausted. However, upon agreement by sovereign States and other parties concerned, settlement of the dispute should be made through arbitration or international adjudication".

98 (1974) 13 ILM 238, 239.

99 GA Res 3281 (1974).

2.4 The State's duties under permanent sovereignty over natural resources

There are also a number of duties espoused under the principle of permanent sovereignty over natural resources. The aim of this section is to highlight some of them. These include: (1) the duty to exercise permanent sovereignty over natural resources for the purposes of national development, (2) the duty to respect the rights of indigenous groups, (3) the duty to treat investors in accordance with international law and (4) the duty to compensate the investor in the event that the State unilaterally terminates a concession agreement.

2.4.1 Duty to exercise permanent sovereignty for national development

Not only do States have the right to exercise permanent sovereignty in the interest of national development, they also have a duty to do so. As such, States have a duty to utilize natural resources within their jurisdiction for the purposes of national development.[100] There is certainly some support for this in international treaties.[101] For example, Article 21(1) of the African Charter on Human and People's Rights, which endorses the principle of permanent sovereignty over natural resources, provides that "This right shall be exercised in the exclusive interest of the people. In no case shall a people be deprived of it". In addition, the African Convention on the Conservation of Nature and Natural Resources of 1968 imposes an obligation on States to "adopt scientifically based conservation, utilization and management plans of forests and rangeland, taking into account the social and economic needs of the States concerned".

Moreover, in the Treaty for Amazonian Co-operation of 1978 there is a recognition that both socio-economic development and conservation of the environment are inherent responsibilities in the sovereignty of each State. This was further reaffirmed in the Amazon Declaration of 1989 where the signatories to the 1978 Treaty stated:

> Conscious of ... the necessity of using this potential to promote economic and social development of our peoples, we reiterate that our Amazon heritage must be preserved through the rational use of the resources of the region, so that present and future generations may benefit from this legacy of nature ... We reaffirm the sovereign right of each country to manage freely its natural resources, bearing in mind the need for promoting the economic and social development of its people.

100 See Article 7 of the Charter on the Rights and Duties of States.

101 See Article 1(2) of the International Covenant on Economic Social and Cultural Rights, which provides that, "All peoples may, for their own ends, freely dispose of their natural wealth and resources without prejudice to any obligations arising out of international economic co-operation, based upon the principle of mutual benefit, and international law. In no case may a people be deprived of its own means of subsistence".

There appears to be no reference to this duty under arbitral awards or other international jurisprudence. As such, "only cursory evidence can be found that under international law, States have a duty to exercise their right to permanent sovereignty in the interest of national development".[102] Despite the scarcity of treaties and lack of absolute specificity under the CERDS and the virtual absence of case law relating to this duty, we would still contend that this duty has some standing under international law. This is owing to the fact that the duty has support in international treaties and is endorsed by jurists. The duty to utilize natural resources for the purposes of national development is linked to the duty in the next subsection, which is the duty to respect the rights and interests of indigenous groups.

2.4.2 Duty to respect the rights and interests of indigenous groups

Another duty emanating from the doctrine of permanent sovereignty over natural resources is the duty to respect the rights and interests of indigenous groups. This duty is linked to the principle of self-determination from which the doctrine of permanent sovereignty itself emanates.[103] The formulation of the definition of indigenous peoples is somewhat controversial.[104] The Mexican Ambassador Martínez Cobo who was Special Rapporteur in the 1971 study on the Problem of Discrimination Against Indigenous Populations defined indigenous populations in his report as follows:

> Indigenous communities, peoples and nations are those which, having a historical continuity with pre-invasion and pre-colonial societies that developed on their territories, consider themselves distinct from other sectors of the societies now prevailing in those territories, or parts of them, They form at present non-dominant sectors of society and are determined to preserve, develop, and transmit to future generations their ancestral territories, and their ethnic identity, as the basis of their continued existence as peoples, in accordance with their own cultural patterns, social institutions and legal systems.[105]

Another potential definition is contained in Article 1(1) of the Indigenous and Tribal People's Convention. The Convention includes the following within its definition of indigenous peoples:

a tribal peoples in independent countries whose social, cultural and economic conditions distinguish them from other sections of the national community, and whose status is regulated wholly or partially by their own customs or traditions or by special laws or regulations;

102 Schrijver (n 24) 310–311.

103 See generally Patrick Thornberry, "Self Determination, Minorities, Human Rights: A Review of International Instruments" (1989) 38 *International and Comparative Law Quarterly* 867, 868.

104 Schrijver (n 24) 313.

105 UN Doc. E/CN.4/Sub 2/1982/21/Add.1.

b peoples in independent countries who are regarded as indigenous on account of their descent from the populations which inhabited the country, or a geographical region to which the country belongs, at the time of conquest or colonization, or the establishment of present state boundaries, who, irrespective of their legal status, retain some or all of their own social, economic, cultural and political institutions.

An important element according to Article 1(2) is that the group of people must actually regard themselves as "indigenous or tribal". This will be an essential factor in determining whether the Convention applies to a particular group.

Prior to the late 1960s there was very little attention paid to the protection of indigenous peoples. Some notable exceptions to this were the General Assembly Resolution 275 (III) of 1949 dealing with the social problems of "aboriginal populations and other under-developed social groups of the American continent" and the International Labour Organization's Convention Concerning the Protection and Integration of Indigenous and Other Tribal and Semi-Tribal Populations in Independent Countries.[106]

The question only really began to arise in the 1960s during the formulation of human rights law on the discrimination and protection of minorities. There was an inclusion of Article 27 in the United Nations Covenant on Civil and Political Rights which stated that "In those States in which ethnic, religious or linguistic minorities exist, persons belonging to such minorities shall not be denied the right, in community with the other members of their group, to enjoy their own culture, to profess and practice their own religion, or to use their own language". Clearly existing here was an overlap between the rights of minorities and indigenous peoples.[107]

In 1982 a Working Group on Indigenous Populations[108] was established to review the rights of indigenous peoples and to develop standards that would protect the rights of indigenous peoples.[109] This eventually culminated in the Declaration on the Rights of Indigenous Peoples that was adopted in 2007. It outlines the various rights available to indigenous peoples. Article 8(2) of the Declaration places upon the State an obligation to ensure that it takes measures to prevent and redress "any action which has the aim or effect of dispossessing" indigenous peoples "of their lands, territories or resources". In addition, Article 10 of the Declaration prohibits the forced removal of indigenous peoples from their lands or territories. In addition, no relocation is to take place without their "free, prior and informed" consent. Moreover, there must be agreement on just

106 International Labour Organization Convention No. 107 of 1957.

107 See Patrick Thornberry, *International Law and the Rights of Minorities* (OUP 1991) 331.

108 UN Doc. E/RES/1982/34. 9th May 1982.

109 Scrhijver, p. 313

and fair compensation, and the option of return where possible. Article 24 of the Declaration goes on to state that:

1. Indigenous peoples have the right to their traditional medicines and to maintain their health practices, including the conservation of their vital medicinal plants, animals and minerals. Indigenous individuals also have the right to access, without any discrimination, to all social and health services.
2. Indigenous individuals have an equal right to the enjoyment of the highest attainable standard of physical and mental health. States shall take the necessary steps with a view to achieving progressively the full realization of this right.

There was also a recognition that indigenous people have a right to benefit from their natural resources. As such, Article 25 of the Declaration provided that indigenous peoples have the right to maintain and strengthen their spiritual relationship with their traditionally owned or occupied lands territories, waters and coastal seas. They also have the right to uphold their responsibilities to future generations in this regard.

There is also the right to the conservation and protection of the environment and productive capacity of the lands or territories belonging to indigenous peoples. This is provided for in Article 29 of the Declaration. The aforementioned provision also imposes an obligation on States to establish and implement assistance programmes for indigenous persons for such conservation and protection, without discrimination. Indigenous people also have the right to redress for lands, territories and resources that have been taken from them without their prior informed consent. Such redress comes in the form of restitution or just, fair and equitable compensation.

There is also some treaty support for the rights of indigenous people. Initially the rights of indigenous peoples were governed by the International Labour Organization Convention concerning the Protection and Integration of Indigenous and Other Tribal and Semi-Tribal Populations in Independent Countries of 1957.[110] However, a criticism of this Convention is that it preferred an approach that encouraged indigenous peoples to assimilate and integrate rather than remain a distinct group with their own distinct traditions and customs.[111] An example of this approach is contained in Article 12(1) of the Convention stated as follows:

> The populations concerned shall not be removed without their free consent from their habitual territories except in accordance with national laws and regulations for reasons relating to national security, or in the interest of national economic development or of the health of the said populations.

110 ILO Convention No. 107 of 1957.

111 See Catherine Brölmann, René Lefeber and Marjoleine Zeick, *Peoples and Minorities in International Law* (Kluwer 1993).

Subsequently to a meeting of experts in 1985 whose goal was to revise the 1957 Convention, the International Labour Organization (ILO) Convention concerning Indigenous and Tribal Peoples in Independent Countries[112] was promulgated. This Convention took a less assimilationist approach and focussed more on the preservation.[113] There is a plethora of provisions contained within this Convention to substantiate this assertion. For example, Article 13 of the Convention provides that in applying the provisions of the Convention, governments must respect the cultures and spiritual values of the peoples concerned. Moreover, Article 15 of the Convention provides that "The rights of the peoples concerned to the natural resources pertaining to their lands shall be specially safeguarded. These rights include the right of these peoples to participate in the use, management and conservation of these resources".[114]

In addition to this, support for the rights of indigenous peoples is found in the Amazon Declaration of 1989. Here the Council reiterated their full respect for the rights of the indigenous populations of the Amazonian region. Thus, they fully supported all measures aimed at maintaining and preserving the integrity of these groups, their cultures and ecological habitats.[115] Moreover, the Convention Biological Diversity also places an obligation on the State to "respect, preserve and maintain knowledge, innovations and practices of indigenous and local communities".[116] However, they are only obligated to do this, "as far as possible and as appropriate". Furthermore, this obligation is subject to national legislation. Therefore, it gives the State a lot of discretion in how it is to implement this provision.

Another Convention that supports the rights of indigenous populations is the United Nations Convention to Combat Desertification. Article 3(a) of this Convention provides that any decisions on the design and implementation of programmes combatting desertification or to mitigate the effect of drought

112 Convention No. 169 of 1989.

113 Brölmann et al. (n 111) 215.

114 See also Article 16 of the ILO Convention concerning Indigenous and Tribal Peoples in Independent Countries which provides that:

> "1 Subject to the following paragraphs of this Article, the peoples concerned shall not be removed from the lands which they occupy.
>
> 2 Where the relocation of these peoples is considered necessary as an exceptional measure, such relocation shall take place only with their free and informed consent. Where their consent cannot be obtained, such relocation shall take place only following appropriate procedures established by national laws and regulations, including public inquiries where appropriate, which provide the opportunity for effective representation of the peoples concerned."

115 Paragraph 3 of the Amazon Declaration, of May 1989, 28 ILM (1989), pp. 1303–1305, where the Council said that, "we reiterate our full respect for the right of indigenous populations of the Amazonian region to have adopted all measures aimed at maintaining and preserving the integrity of these human groups, their cultures and their ecological habitats, subject to the exercise of the right which is inherent in the sovereignty of each State".

116 See Article 8(j) of the Convention on Biological Diversity.

must be taken with the participation of populations and local communities. Article 5(d) of the Convention further provides that States must promote awareness and facilitate the participation of local populations in their efforts to combat desertification and mitigate the effects of drought. Article 19(1)(a) also provides that any capacity-building activities, education and public awareness in combating of desertification must include the full participation of local organizations.[117]

In addition to treaties and conventions, support for the rights of indigenous peoples under international law is found in international case law. Thus, in the *Western Sahara Case*[118] the International Court of Justice opined that territories in which socially and politically organized tribes lived were not to be regarded as terra nullius nor were they free to be occupied and acquired at a whim.[119] This represents a recognition that the rights of indigenous people are to be respected and that self-determination should be pursued.[120]

Protection of the rights of indigenous people's is still an emerging area under international law. However, from the international law sources espoused, it is clear that States have some obligations to protect the collective rights of indigenous peoples to land and natural resources.[121] It is even contended that as a result, some of these rights now form a part of customary international law. They further redefine the international investment law, which is more "state-centred" and recognizes that there is a positive obligation to guarantee the rights of indigenous peoples to natural resources and participatory collective rights.[122]

2.4.3 The duty to treat investors in accordance with international law

Whilst the State has the right to exercise authority over foreign investment and to regulate it, there is also duty to exercise this right in accordance with international law. Thus, when it comes to nationalization, for example, there are certain international law principles that must be observed. Not only should the nationalization be for a public purpose, it should also be non-discriminatory and must be accompanied by the payment of compensation. Moreover, nationalization may also be rendered illegal if carried out in breach of a treaty.[123] This subsection examines these factors, in turn.

117 See also Article 1(j) of the International Tropical Timber Agreement 1994, which lists as one of its objectives, "To encourage members to support and develop industrial tropical timber reforestation and forest management activities as well as rehabilitation of degraded forest land, with due regard for the interests of local communities dependent on forest resources".

118 Advisory Opinion Western Sahara (1975) ICJ Reports 12, 35–37.

119 Schrijver (n 24) 318.

120 Advisory Opinion (n 118) 68.

121 Ricardo Pereira and Orla Gough, "Permanent Sovereignty over Natural Resources in the 21st Century: Natural Resource Governance and the Right to Self-Determination of Indigenous Peoples under International Law" (2013) 14 *Melbourne Journal of International Law* 1, 44.

122 Ibid.

123 See Rudolf Dolzer and Christoph Schreuer, *Principles of International Investment Law* (2nd edn, OUP, 2012) 99–101.

2.4.3.1 Public purpose

It is clear from the various resolutions and the definition of nationalization that it must be for a public purpose.[124] If the nationalization is not for public purpose then it will be rendered illegal even if compensation is paid.[125] Thus, in the case of *Sabbatino v Banco Nacional de Cuba*[126] the nationalization was rendered illegal because the public purpose element was missing. This however can be contrasted with the case of *Libyan American Oil Company (LIAMCO) v Libya*[127] where the tribunal opined that:

> As to the contention that the said measures were politically motivated and not in pursuance of a legitimate public purpose, it is the general opinion in international theory that the public utility principle is not a necessary requisite for the legality of a nationalization.[128]

Despite the contrast in views, nationalization without public purpose is difficult to envisage. This is owing to the fact that nationalization by its very nature subsumes public purpose.[129] As such, it would not qualify as a nationalization if it is not for a public purpose. For this reason it has been advanced that "public purpose is one of the elements definitive of an expropriation rather than a requirement for lawful expropriations".[130]

What is not so clear is the precise definition of "public purpose". Indeed the early case of *Certain German Interests in the Polish Upper Silesia* made an attempt at propounding a definition of public purpose. As such, the Permanent Court of International Justice defined it as, "reasons of public utility, judicial liquidation and similar measures".[131] Although this definition could lead to some confusion one could also interpret it very widely. This is advantageous because it then leaves it to the State to determine what amounts to a public purpose. This view is supported in the case of *James v United Kingdom*[132] where the European Court of Human Rights held that since "the margin of appreciation available to the legislature in implementing social and economic policies should be a wide one", the Court respected their judgement as to what constitutes the "public interest".

124 Permanent Sovereignty over Natural Resources, G.A. Res. 1803 (XVII), U.N. Doc.A/5217 (Dec. 14, 1962).

125 Dunia P. Zongwe, "The Contribution of Campbell v Zimbabwe to the Foreign Investment Law on Expropriations" (2010) 2 *Namibia Law Journal* 31, 37.

126 (1961) 193 F Supp. 375 at 38.

127 (1977) 63 ILR 140. See also the *Shufeldt Claim* (1930) UNRIAA 1079 at 1095 "[I]t is perfectly competent for the Government of Guatemala to enact any decree they like and for any reasons they see fit, and such reasons are no concern of the Tribunal".

128 Ibid.

129 Zongwe (125) 38.

130 Ibid.

131 *Certain German Interests in Polish Upper Silesia*, 1926 PCIJ, Series A, No. 7, p. 2.

132 *James v United Kingdom* (1986) 8 EHRR 123.

The European Court of Human Rights would only question such judgement, if it was "manifestly without reasonable foundation".[133]

2.4.3.2 Non-discriminatory

Nationalization will also be deemed illegal if it is discriminatory. Discrimination is very much about the action of the perpetrator.[134] It could be motivated by either prejudice or discriminatory intent, be motivated by factors other than prejudice or be an action which has the effect of disproportionately disadvantaging a particular group of people.

There are a number of examples, in case law, illustrating the illegality of discrimination under international investment law. For example, in the case of *Siderman de Blake v. Argentina*,[135] the Argentinian government nationalized a hotel on the basis that its owners were Jewish. This was held to be illegal because it was discriminatory. Similarly, in the case of *Mike Campbell (Pvt) Ltd and Others v Zimbabwe*[136] the Southern African Development Community (SADC) Tribunal held that the Zimbabwean government's nationalization of white-owned farms was illegal because it was racially motivated.

2.4.3.3 Breach of a treaty

Nationalization will also be deemed illegal if it is carried out in breach of a treaty. This essentially means that if the nationalization is carried out in a manner that contravenes provisions of a treaty that the host State has entered into, then this will be deemed illegal. Thus, in the case of *Certain German Interests in the Polish Upper Silesia*, Poland had nationalized a nitrate factory that belonged to a German national. According to Article 6 of the Geneva Convention Concerning Upper Silesia, Poland was prohibited from nationalizing assets belonging to German nationals in Upper Silesia. The Permanent Court of International Justice held that the nationalization here was illegal because it was in breach of a treaty. Therefore, it can be seen that in event that a nationalization is in breach of a treaty then this will render it illegal.

2.4.8 The duty to pay compensation

In order for nationalization to be legal the host State must pay compensation.[137] In the *Upton Case*,[138] which arose out of Venezuela's expropriation of American

133 Ibid paragraph 46.
134 See Christopher McCrudden, *Anti-Discrimination Law* (Dartmouth 1991).
135 965 F. 2d 699 (1992) 712–713.
136 SADC (T) Case No. 2/2007.
137 Muna Ndulo, "The Nationalization of the Zambian Copper Industry" (1974) 6 *Zambia Law Journal* 55, 65.
138 (1903) Ven Arbitr., 173.

property, the arbitral tribunal opined that States have the right to appropriate private property for public purpose. However, they have an obligation to compensate the owner in such an event.[139] The purpose of compensation is to, as far as possible, wipe out all of the consequences of the nationalization. Therefore, the compensation is to "re-establish the situation which would have existed if the act had not been committed".[140]

What is not so clear is the standard of compensation payable to the investor. It would appear that there are two standards of compensation under international investment law. These are the Hull Principle and the appropriate compensation standard. These two standards will be discussed in greater detail in Chapter 4. However, for the purposes of introduction, under the Hull Principle, compensation payable must be prompt, adequate and effective. Prompt means that there should be no inordinate delays.[141] Adequate means that the compensation must restore the investor to a position that they would have been in had the State not abrogated the concession. This not only includes payment for sunk costs (*damnum emergens*) but also for lost future profits (*lucrum cessans*).[142] Effective means that the compensation must be paid in a freely convertible currency.[143]

2.5 Conclusion

It could thus be concluded that the principle of permanent sovereignty over natural resources espouses that States have the right to do whatever they wish with minerals found within their jurisdiction. This doctrine was born after the Second World War, when mineral-rich nations who started to acquire their political independence also sought to acquire economic independence. In so doing they wished to exert more authority on their natural resources.

There are many rights arising out of the doctrine of permanent sovereignty over natural resources. This book mainly focusses on: (1) The right to freely dispose of natural resources, (2) the right to explore and exploit natural resources freely, (3) the right to use natural resources for development and (4) the right to regulate foreign investment. Furthermore, it was highlighted that there are a number of duties emanating from the principle. These include (1) the duty to exercise permanent sovereignty over natural resources for the purposes of national development, (2) the duty to respect the rights of indigenous groups, (3) the duty to treat investors in accordance with international law and

139 Ibid 194.

140 *Case concerning German interests in Upper Silesia*, P.C.I.J. Series, A, Nos. 7, 9, 17, 19 (1926–29). See also generally Markus Burgstaller and Jonathan Ketcheson, "Should Expropriation Risk Be Taken into Account in the Assessment of Damages" (2017) 32 *ICSID Review* 193, 198–207.

141 Rudolf Dolzer and Margrete Stevens, *Bilateral Investment Treaties* (Martinus Nijhoff 1995) 112.

142 See *Sapphire International v National Iranian Oil Company* (1963) 35 ILR 136, 186.

143 Ibid.

(4) the duty to compensate the investor in the event that the State unilaterally terminates a concession agreement. Thus it can be seen that in as much as the State has many rights under the doctrine of permanent sovereignty over natural resources, this comes with a number of duties.

The doctrine of permanent sovereignty is important because it is the basis upon which host States enter into concession agreements with foreign investors. It is also important because it is frequently invoked, when host States choose to unilaterally terminate such concession agreements. Given the administrative and legislative prerogatives at the disposal of the host State, investors seek to ensure that they do not use these in order to adversely affect the latter's contractual rights within the concession. As such, investors often insist on the insertion of stabilization clauses. These are inserted to ensure that the State do not utilize these prerogatives and to ensure that the agreement subsists for the duration stipulated in the concession. The purpose of the next chapter is to discuss the effect of stabilization clauses in concession agreements.

3 Political risk and the effect of stabilization clauses in concession agreements

3.1 Introduction

The preceding chapter discussed the principle of permanent sovereignty over natural resources. Under this principle, host States have the right to freely explore and exploit the natural resources found within their jurisdiction.[1] The principle of permanent sovereignty over natural resources is the basis upon which States enter into concession agreements with foreign investors.[2] Such agreements are invariably long-term in nature. Typically, under these agreements, the investor is to use its capital and technical know-how to explore and exploit the host State's natural resources. In return, the investor is to pay the host State royalties and taxes, typically at a preferential rate.[3]

One of the major concerns is the stability of the actual agreements, once the investment is sunk. This is owing to the fact that the State has a plethora of prerogatives at its disposal. It could use these in a manner that could adversely affect the investor. Investors are at particular risk, in the advanced stages of the resource nationalism cycle. This occurs when the natural resource experiences a sustained upward trend. In such circumstances, the host State seeks to maximize the benefits accruing from its natural resource. This is accomplished either through revising any tax incentives that the investor has previously enjoyed or through the outright nationalization of the investor's assets. As such, the stability of the concession agreement is primary concern of the investor.[4]

In order to ensure the credibility of their agreements, host States and investors will agree to the insertion of stabilization clauses in concession agreements.[5]

1 General Assembly Resolution 1803 (XXVII) of 14 December 1962.

2 Sangwani Patrick Ng'ambi, "Permanent Sovereignty over Natural Resources and the Sanctity of Contracts, From the Angle of Lucrum Cessans" (2015) 12 *Loyola University Chicago International Law Review* 153, 159.

3 See generally Kojo Yelpaala, "In Search of Effective Policies for Foreign Direct Investment: Alternatives to Tax Incentive Policies" (1985) 7 *Northwestern Journal of International Law and Business* 208.

4 Rudolf Dolzer and Christoph Schreuer, *Principles of International Investment Law* (2nd edn, OUP 2012) 82–83.

5 Sam F. Halabi, "Efficient Contracting between Foreign Investors and Host States: Evidence from Stabilization Clauses" (2011) 31 *Northwestern Journal of International Law and Business* 261, 290.

Stabilization clauses are undertakings on the part of the host State that it will not take any administrative or legislative actions that would adversely affect the contractual interests of the investor.[6] The purpose of these clauses is to ensure that the concession subsists for the timeframe stipulated therein. Section 3.2 looks at political risk under international investment law. It covers aspects such as the resource nationalism cycle and the means through which host States protect themselves from its effects. Section 3.3 looks at stabilization clauses including the types in existence and the case law pertaining to stabilization clauses. Section 3.4 will consist of a conclusion.

3.2 Mitigating political risk in international investment law

At the time of signing a concession, there exists an asymmetrical relationship between host State and the investor. This asymmetrical relationship exists as a result of the myriad legislative and administrative prerogatives that the State has at its disposal. These prerogatives could be employed by the State, in a way that is calculated to jeopardize the investor's prospects of making a profit once it actually sends its capital. The State could, for example, prematurely terminate the contract and nationalize assets belonging to the investor by utilizing the legislative process.[7] Similarly, they could raise taxes which could either have the effect of significantly reducing the investor's profits or simply make it more onerous or expensive to run operations in a given jurisdiction.[8]

Premature termination or alteration of the mining agreements could have a huge impact on the mining operations. This is owing to the fact that, in the first instance, commencing with an exploration project in resource-rich countries can be very expensive and laborious. Mining and oil companies alike almost invariably explore various areas before they eventually attain success. Once they do, they will need to make up for the shortfall created by the failed projects. In addition, mineral prices are somewhat mercurial in that they tend to fluctuate and depreciate owing to a plethora of factors that are beyond the scope of this book.[9]

With this much uncertainty in the venture, it is understandable therefore that any additional uncertainties in this equation are unlikely to render the business venture unprofitable.[10] Predictability in the law, particularly the fiscal regime, is therefore imperative factors in determining to whether the investor will sign a

6 Junji Nakagawa, *Nationalization, Natural Resources and International Investment Law: Contractual Relationship as a Dynamic Bargaining Process* (Routledge 2018) 11.

7 Abdullah Faruque, "Validity and Efficacy of Stabilization Clauses: Legal Protection vs Functional Value" (2006) 23 *Journal of International Arbitration* 317.

8 Joseph Nwaokoro, "Enforcing Stabilization of International Energy Contracts" (2013) 3 *Journal of World Energy Law & Business* 103, 104.

9 See generally Thomas W. Waelde and George Ndi, "Stabilizing International Investment Commitments: International Law Versus Contract Interpretation" (1996) 31 *Texas International Law Journal* 215, 223–226.

10 Ibid 227.

concession.[11] The investor will therefore insist on some assurances that the sanctity of contract is respected and that they will be guaranteed against the arbitrary exercise of State power which will alter or unilaterally abrogate their contractual rights.[12] Section 3.2.1 will look at the resource nationalism cycle and the factors contributing to it. Section 3.2.2 will look at the types of protections employed in order for investors to insulate themselves from the effects of the resource nationalism cycle, including stabilization clauses.

3.2.1 The resource nationalism cycle

Once investors commence operations in the host State, they are exposed to a number of risks.[13] Typically, these risks manifest in the advanced stages of the resource nationalism cycle.[14] The cycle typically begins with the host State soliciting foreign investment and ultimately granting a concession to a foreign investor. It typically ends when the host government seeks to exert greater control over its natural resources, subsequently to the commencement of operations. This could either come in the form of increased taxation or outright nationalization of the investor's assets.

Resource-rich nations invariably solicit foreign direct investment, because they do not have the necessary capital or technical know-how that is needed, in order to explore and exploit their natural resources. Foreign direct investment is used as a means of attracting much needed capital to the host State.[15] In order to attract investors, host States structure their policy towards creating an investor-friendly environment. This is accomplished by liberalizing the economy and introducing tax incentives into their standard concession agreements.

Standard concession agreements are structured in a way that allows the investor to run operations and generate their profits. The concession agreements also provide that the investor is expected to pay taxes and royalties to the host State. At the time that the terms are being negotiated, the prices of the host State's natural resources are typically quite low.[16] Furthermore, industry may be experiencing a decline that can only be remedied by foreign capital. At that point the State is the weaker party and may be compelled to acquiesce in the investor's request for contractual and fiscal incentives.[17] Once the investment is sunk and operations

11 Faruque (n 7) 322.

12 Muthucumaraswamy Sornarajah, *The Settlement of Foreign Investment Disputes* (Kluwer 2000) 49.

13 See Sangwani Patrick Ng'ambi, "Mineral Taxation and Resource Nationalism in Zambia" (2015) 2 *Southern African Journal of Policy and Development* 6.

14 See generally Thomas W. Wälde, "Renegotiating Acquired Rights in the Oil and Gas Industries: Industry and Political Cycles Meet the Rule of Law" (2008) 1 *Journal of World Energy Law and Business* 55.

15 James C. Baker, *Foreign Direct Investment in Less Developed Countries: The Role of ICSID and MIGA* (Quorum Books 1999) 5.

16 Wälde, (n 14) 55.

17 Thomas W. Waelde and George Ndi, "Stabilizing International Investment Commitments: International Law Versus Contract Interpretation" (1996) 31 *Texas International Law Journal* 215, 223.

commence, the investor eventually becomes the weaker party, because the host State has a number of legislative and administrative prerogatives at its disposal. This is what is referred to as the obsolescing bargaining model.[18] This model basically hypothesizes that concession agreements are susceptible to later changes by the host State once operations have commenced.[19] This is certainly the case once the price of the natural resource experiences a sustained upward trend.

Once prices of the natural resource experience a sustained upward trend, the popular perception is that the foreign investor is making a larger profit, much to the detriment of the people of the host State. This may prompt the host State to exert greater control over the natural resources. As such they will seek to maximize the benefits accruing from these windfall profits, which may involve rescinding any fiscal incentives granted, or outrightly nationalizing the investment.

Resource nationalism is not only influenced by increased prices.[20] The system of governance of the host State is also a factor contributing to whether it takes a resource nationalist stance and implements that agenda. Resource nationalism will typically manifest in host States where political pressure exists through regular elections and where there are few checks and balances on the sitting government.[21] An authoritarian system is likely to adopt a resource nationalist stance. Despite the fact that an authoritarian system has fewer checks and balances, there are no elections. This means that there is no political pressure on the executive. As such, it is easier for the government to ignore the socio-economic needs of the people living in the host State.[22] Furthermore, authoritarian States do not shy away from using the mechanisms at their disposal, in order to quash popular dissent against foreign investors.[23] The only time an authoritarian State may adopt resource nationalist policies is when their political hegemony is threatened.

A democratic regime is the least likely of the political systems to adopt a resource nationalist stance. Political pressure certainly exists in a democratic system. This often manifests through regular elections. However, a functional democracy also has checks and balances which means that there are mechanisms to ameliorate political risk.[24] This means that it has strong and independent

18 See generally Raymond Vernon, *Sovereignty at Bay: The Multinational Spread of US Enterprises* (Longman 1971).

19 Ibid.

20 Ekim Arbtali, "Political Regimes, Investment Risk and Resource Nationalism: An Empirical Analysis" 21, http://regconf.hse.ru/uploads/7da62134fab330f54f067e5cd2e603c40298cd7e.pdf.

21 See Sergei Guriev, Anton Kolotilin and Konstantin Sonin, "Determinants of Nationalization in the Oil Sector: A Theory and Evidence from Panel Data" (2009) 27 *The Journal of Law, Economics, & Organization* 301.

22 Geoffrey Garrett and Peter Lange, "Internationalization, Institutions and Political Change" in Robert O. Keohane and Helen V. Milner (eds), *Internationalization and Domestic Politics* (Cambridge University Press 1996) 48, 61 and Paul Brooker, *Non-Democratic Regimes: Theory, Government and Politics* (Macmillan 2000) 167–169.

23 Quan Li, "Democracy, Autocracy and Expropriation of Foreign Direct Investment" (2009) 42 *Comparative Political Studies* 1098, 1106.

24 Nathan M. Jensen, *Nation-States and the Multinational Corporation* (Princeton 2006) 80.

judicial and legislative wings.[25] As such, in the event that the host State acts in a manner that adversely affects the interests of the investor, the other wings of government are in a position to scrutinize the actions of the executive.[26]

A hybrid system is the one that most likely to adopt a resource nationalist stance and can quite easily implement that agenda. There are three key features that characterize a hybrid system. These are:

> highly centralized state authority concentrated in the executive branch; formal institutions of democracy, including room for at least some candidates to oppose incumbent authorities on the ballot in elections to powerful posts; and the systematic gutting of these institutions and their frequent functional replacement by substitutions—often either outside the constitutional framework or in violation of the spirit of the constitution—that are created by and highly dependent on central authorities.[27]

Therefore, this is a system where the executive is still accountable to the people through regular elections. As such, political pressure exists. However, a hybrid system does not have the same checks and balances that are typically found in a functional democracy. Thus, the host State is more likely to implement a resource nationalist agenda, as they would be influenced by the need to retain power in the next election. Moreover, there are no institutional mechanisms preventing them from implementing such an agenda.

It is also postulated that resource nationalism is an expression of "nationalism" rather than an expression of "socialism".[28] Host States nationalize as a means of imprinting a national identity on its industries. For example, when the government of Zambia nationalized its mining operations in the 1970s, this was owing to the fact that economic activity in Zambia was dominated by foreigners.[29] Thus, the aim of the government was to "Zambianize" such businesses.[30] It also proceeded to obtain a 51% equity stake in all companies, including those in the mining industry.[31] As such, it can be seen that nationalism was the pretext of the nationalisms that occurred in Zambia in the 1970s.[32]

25 Larry Diamond, *Developing Democracy: Toward Consolidation* (Johns Hopkins 1999) 11, Philippe C. Schmitter and Terry Lynn Karl, "What Democracy Is. . . and Is Not" (1991) 2 *Journal of Democracy* 75, 76.

26 See Nathan Jensen, "Political Risk, Democratic Institutions and Foreign Direct Investment" (2008) 70 *The Journal of Politics* 1040.

27 Nikolai Petrov, Masha Lipman and Henry H. Hale, *Overmanaged Democracy in Russia: Governance Implications of Hybrid Regimes* (Carnegie Endowment for International Peace 2010) 3.

28 Amy Chua, "The Privatization-Nationalization Cycle: The Link between Markets and Ethnicity in Developing Countries" (1995) 95 *Columbia Law Review* 95, 262.

29 Andrew Sardanis, *Africa: Another Side of the Coin: Northern Rhodesia's Final Years and Zambia's Nationhood* (I.B. Tauris 2011) 212.

30 Ibid.

31 Marcia Burdette, "Nationalization in Zambia: A Critique of Bargaining Theory" (1977) 11 *Canadian Journal of African Studies* 471, 480.

32 Ibid.

The difficulty, however, with eliminating foreign nationals from the picture is that this also eliminates their foreign capital.[33] The anti-foreigner euphoria is often succeeded by severe economic problems. This is typically caused by mismanagement and depreciation of the price of the natural resources. Consequently, industry declines. To resuscitate the industry, host States typically have to solicit foreign capital, which means seeking out foreign investors.[34] This thus brings the host State right back to the early stages of the resource nationalism cycle.

3.2.2 Protections against the resource nationalism cycle

Investors employ various means of mitigating the risks associated with the resource nationalism cycle.[35] This can be accomplished through political risk insurance. Under such schemes, the investor is indemnified against any non-business risks associated with investing in mineral-rich nations. Protections are also afforded through bilateral and multilateral treaties. Such treaties contain provisions pertaining to the protection of foreign investors. For example, Bilateral Investment Treaties (BITs) contain umbrella clauses, which require "each Contracting State to observe all investment obligations that it has assumed with respect to investors from the other Contracting State".[36] They also have provisions pertaining to nationalization and the standard of compensation applicable. Investors also protect themselves through contractual clauses that are inserted in concession agreements: for example, they invariably insert arbitration clauses into concession agreements. Such clauses essentially ensure that in the event that a dispute arises between the host State and investor, then it will be decided by a neutral forum which is operating above the fray of the national mechanisms of the host State. Tied to this is the choice of law clause, which ensures that a law other than that of the host State will govern the contractual provisions of the concession agreement. Finally, investors may also consider inserting renegotiation clauses and stabilization clauses. The former places an obligation on the host State and the investor to renegotiate the terms of the concession agreement, in the event that circumstances change. The latter clause is a way of ensuring that the State does not use its legislative or administrative prerogatives to unilaterally abrogate the contract.[37]

33 Chua n (28) 262.

34 Ibid.

35 Abul F.M. Maniruzzaman, "The Issue of Resource Nationalism: Risk Engineering and Dispute Management in the Oil and Gas Industry" (2009) 5 *Journal of Oil and Gas Law* 79, 99.

36 Jarrod Wong, "Umbrella Clauses in Bilateral Investment Treaties: Of Breaches of Contract, Treaty Violations, and the Divide between Developing and Developed Countries in Foreign Investment Disputes" (2006) 14 *George Mason Law Review* 137, 144.

37 Surya Subedi, *International Investment Law: Reconciling Policy and Principle* (2nd edn, Hart Publishing 2012) 101.

3.2.2.1 Political risk insurance

One means through which investors protect themselves against the consequences of the resource nationalism cycle is through political risk insurance. There is a plethora of organizations providing this sort of insurance. The public ones include Overseas Private Insurance Corporation (OPIC) and the Multilateral Investment Guarantee Agency (MIGA). Among the private ones are the American Insurance Group (AIG), Lloyds of London, Sovereign Risk Insurance Limited, Chubb and Zurich Emerging Markets Solution.[38]

OPIC operates with the backing of the US government.[39] It operates on a self-sustaining basis.[40] Consequently, the organization has recorded a profit for every year it has operated since inception. OPIC is targeted at helping American investors. As such, OPIC "helps U.S. businesses invest overseas, fosters economic development in new and emerging markets, complements the private sector in managing risks associated with foreign direct investment, and supports U.S. foreign policy".[41] The major advantage of obtaining insurance under OPIC is that it provides protection to investors' assets for up to twenty years. This is significantly longer than its private counterparts.[42] In addition to this, OPIC may also authorize loans.[43]

Another publicly backed investment insurance scheme is MIGA. MIGA operates under the auspices of the World Bank. It was established in 1988, and the main reason for its existence is to protect the flow of foreign investment to developing countries.[44] According to Article 11 of the Convention Establishing the Multilateral Investment Guarantee Agency (MIGA Convention), MIGA provides cover for non-business risks, such as nationalization, war or civil disturbance, breach of contract and any losses arising from any introduction of restrictions on the transfer of currency outside the State. Article 12 of the MIGA Convention covers eligible types of investment. These are equity interests, non-equity direct investment and any medium- or long-term forms of investment. In addition to this, in order for the investment to be eligible, it must be made into a developing country. This is as provided for in Article 14 of the MIGA Convention.

3.2.2.2 Bilateral and multilateral treaties

Investors are also protected through the bilateral and multilateral treaties to which their home States are signatories. These treaties contain within them various provisions which afford protection to foreign investors. For example, most

38 Maniruzzaman (n 35), 99.

39 Ashton B. Inniss, "Rethinking Political Risk Insurance: Incentives for Investor Risk Mitigation" (2010) 16 *Southwestern Journal of International Law* 477, 488.

40 Overseas Private Investment Corporation, OPIC Handbook (2006) 4, http://www.opic.gov/sites/default/files/docs/OPIC_Handbook.pdf.

41 Ibid.

42 Inniss, (n 39) 489.

43 Ibid.

44 See Article 2 of the Convention Establishing the Multilateral Investment Guarantee Agency.

multilateral treaties concerning foreign investment contain clauses protecting investors against nationalization without compensation. An example of this is Article 1110 of the North American Free Trade Agreement. This agreement provides that no Party may directly or indirectly nationalize assets belonging to an investor of another party in its territory unless it is for a public purpose, non-discriminatory, in accordance with due process of law and is accompanied with compensation.[45] BITs also have similar provisions dealing with nationalization. An example of this is contained in Article 4(1) of the Chinese Model Bilateral Investment Treaty (2003) which provides that:

> Neither Contracting Party shall expropriate, nationalize or take other similar measures (hereinafter referred to as "expropriation") against the investments of the investors of the other Contracting Party in its territory, unless the following conditions are met:
> a for the public interests;
> b under domestic legal procedure;
> c without discrimination;
> d against compensation.

BITs also contain "umbrella clauses" within them. Umbrella clauses are provisions found in treaties, requiring the Contracting State to observe all investment obligations it assumes in relation to an investor from another Contracting State.[46] These are found in many free trade agreements (FTAs) and bilateral investment treaties BITs.[47] The general purpose behind this clause is to ensure that any arbitral tribunal constituted under the auspices of the FTA or BIT have direct jurisdiction over any claims for breach of agreement. This is owing to the fact that a breach of agreement also amounts to a breach of the umbrella clause.[48]

45 See also Article 13 of the Energy Charter Treaty which has a similar provision. It says that, "(1) Investments of Investors of a Contracting Party in the Area of any other Contracting Party shall not be nationalized, expropriated or subjected to a measure or measures having effect equivalent to nationalization or expropriation (hereinafter referred to as "Expropriation") except where such Expropriation is:

a for a purpose which is in the public interest;
b not discriminatory;
c carried out under due process of the law; and
d accompanied by the payment of prompt, adequate and effective compensation.

Such compensation shall amount to the fair market value of the Investment expropriated at the time immediately before the Expropriation or impending Expropriation became known in such a way as to affect the value of the Investment (hereinafter referred to as the "Valuation Date").

Such fair market value shall at the request of the Investor be expressed in a Freely Convertible Currency on the basis of the market rate of exchange existing for that currency on the Valuation Date. Compensation shall also include interest at a commercial rate established on a market basis from the date of Expropriation until the date of payment".

46 Wong (n 36) 144.

47 Ibid. See also Nakagawa (n 6) 207.

48 Ibid.

These clauses are by no means new. An early example of these umbrella clause is contained in the 1959 BIT between Germany and Pakistan. In an address to the German Parliament, the German Government stated that "The violation of such an obligation [of an investment agreement] accordingly will also amount to a violation of the international legal obligation contained in the present Treaty".[49]

Umbrella clauses arose out of a need to protect investments, which would otherwise be subject to the municipal law of the host State, which may sometimes be drafted in a way that adversely effects the investor. This particularly became an issue of concern after 1945, a period which saw an increase in large-scale foreign investments. This necessitated the use of umbrella clauses, which act as a bridge between contractual arrangements, the domestic law of the host State and international law, which, in turn, allows for increased investor security.[50] The umbrella clause thus protects the contract and is an expression of the principle of *pacta sunt servanda*. Thus, any breach of an umbrella clause is a breach of international law.[51]

There is a plethora of examples of umbrella clauses contained in BITs. An example of this is Article 2(2) of the British Model Treaty which says that "Each Contracting Party shall observe any obligation it may have entered into with regard to investments of nationals or companies of the other Contracting Party".[52] Article III of the investment protection Treaty entered into between France and Hong Kong in 1995 stated that:

> Without prejudice to the provisions of this Agreement, each Contracting Party Shall observe any particular obligation it may have entered into with regard to investments of investors of the other Contracting Party, including provisions more favourable than those of this Agreement.

The precise application of these clauses remains in a state of flux. Some arbitral tribunals have affirmed the application of umbrella clauses. However, some have adopted a more restrictive approach to them. There are a number of cases that give full effect to umbrella clauses. One of these is the case of *SGS v Philippines*[53] which concerned an umbrella clause in a BIT between Switzerland and the Philippines. The arbitral tribunal held that a breach of Article X(2), which was the umbrella clause, was a violation of the BIT.[54] As such the tribunal stated that failure of the host State to observe its binding commitments, including contractual commitments, constitutes a breach of the bilateral investment Treaty.[55]

49 Translation taken from Dolzer and Schreuer (n 4) 167.
50 Dolzer and Schreuer (n 4) 168.
51 Ibid.
52 Dolzer and Schreuer (n 4) 167.
53 Decision on Jurisdiction, 29 January 2004, 8 ICSID Reports 518, 42 ILM (2003) 138.
54 Paragraph 119.
55 Paragraph 128.

The tribunal stated, however, that the umbrella clause "does not convert the issue of the extent or content of such obligations into an issue of international law".[56] That issues was still to be governed by the investment agreement.[57]

In the case of *Noble Ventures v Romania*[58] the ICSID Tribunal was tasked with interpreting and applying Article II(2)(c) of the BIT between the United States and Romania. Article II(2)(c) stated that "Each party shall observe any obligation it may have entered into with regard to investments". Counsel for the US claimant contended, among other things, that Romania had failed to abide by its contractual obligation to renegotiate the debts of a formerly state-owned company, acquired by the investor. In so doing, this constituted a breach of the umbrella clause. The tribunal held that:

> Two States may include in a bilateral investment treaty a provision to the effect that, in the interest of achieving the objects and goals of the treaty, the host State may incur international responsibility by reason of a breach of its contractual obligations towards the private investor of the other Party, the breach of contract being thus "internationalized", i.e. assimilated to a breach of the treaty.[59]

In their view, the aim of the parties in including Article II(2)(c) in the BIT was to equate contractual obligations, which would typically be governed by the municipal law, to Treaty obligations as established in the BIT. Because of the inclusion of the umbrella clause, the tribunal thus considered the Claimant's claims for breach of contract on the basis that any such breach constituted a breach of the BIT.[60] The ICSID Tribunal ultimately found that Romania had not breach its contractual obligation. Further, the Tribunal left open the question of whether the wide scope of an umbrella clause ought to be narrowed.

The case of *Eureko v Poland*[61] concerned the interpretation of an umbrella clause in Article 3.5 of the Treaty between the Netherlands and Poland. In making their determination, the tribunal considered the ordinary meaning, the context of the clause and the maxim of *effet utile* in arriving at a determination. The Tribunal opined that by breaching its obligations under the contract, this could effectively amount to a breach of the BIT's umbrella clause. This is despite the fact that Poland did not violate the BITs other standards. The tribunal thus opined that:

> The plain meaning – the 'ordinary meaning' - of a provision prescribing that a State 'shall observe any obligation it may have entered into' with regard to certain foreign investment is not obscure. The phrase, 'shall observe' is

56 Ibid.
57 Ibid.
58 ICSID Case No. ARB/01/11.
59 Paragraph 64.
60 Paragraphs 61–62.
61 Partial Award, 18 August 2005, 12 ICSID Reports 273.

> imperative and categorical. 'Any' obligation is capacious; it means not only obligations of a certain type, but "any" - that is to say, all – obligations entered into with regard to investments of investors of the other Contracting Party …[62]

The claim in *SGS v Paraguay*[63] concerned unpaid bills under a contract for the pre-shipment inspection of goods, between the investor and the State. The umbrella clause was contained in Article 11 of the BIT between Switzerland and Paraguay. It stated that "[e]ither Contracting Party shall constantly guarantee the observance of the commitments it has entered into with respect to the investments of the investors of the other Contracting Party". The tribunal refused to adopt a restrictive interpretation of the umbrella clause, based either on the type of contract or type of breach at hand. As such the tribunal said commercial contracts were well within the scope of Article 11.[64] The ICSID Tribunal further stated that:

> Likewise, Article 11 does not state that its constant guarantee of observance of such commitments may be breached only through actions that a commercial company cannot take, through abuses of state power, or through exertions of undue government influence.[65]

The tribunal further opined that the obligation under Article 11 is to observe commitments. In their view, failure to observe obligations under the contract constitutes a failure to observe one's commitments. Nothing in Article 11 suggested that "a government will only fail to observe its commitments if it abuses its sovereign authority".[66] The tribunal in this case thus gave full effect to the umbrella clause. This would suggest that breach of obligations incidental to investments also amounts to a breach of a Treaty.[67]

There is also some case law which gives a narrow interpretation to umbrella clauses. The first case is that of *SGS v Pakistan*.[68] This case concerned the interpretation of the umbrella clause in the Swiss-Pakistan BIT. Pakistan had entered into a contact on pre-shipment inspection services with SGS. When Pakistan unilaterally terminated this contract, the claimant initiated arbitral proceedings under ICSID, on the basis of the BIT. The umbrella clause in the BIT stated that "Either Contracting Party shall constantly guarantee the observance of the commitments it has entered into with respect to investments of the investors of

62 Paragraph 246.
63 Decision on Jurisdiction, 12 February 2010, ICSID Case No. ARB/07/29.
64 *SGS v Paraguay*, Decision on Jurisdiction, 12 February 2010, ICSID Case No. ARB/07/29, paragraph 168.
65 *SGS v Paraguay*, Decision on Jurisdiction, 12 February 2010, paragraph 68.
66 *SGS v Paraguay*, Award, 10 February 2012, paragraph 91.
67 Dolzer and Schreuer (n 4) 171.
68 Decision on Jurisdiction, CASE No. ARB/01/13, 6 August 2003.

the other Contracting Party". The tribunal held that there was nothing in the wording of the umbrella clause to suggest that State breaches of a contract "are automatically 'elevated' to the level of breaches of international law.[69] Elevating a contract to this level would open the floodgates and would mean that breach of a number of other State contracts, currently governed by municipal law, would also amount to a breach of the BIT.[70]

Another case in which umbrella clause was interpreted narrowly was that of *Joy Mining Machinery Limited v The Arabic Republic of Egypt*.[71] The dispute here concerned *inter alia* the interpretation of an umbrella clause under the UK-Egypt BIT. The tribunal held that the umbrella clause does not have the effect of transforming all contractual disputes into investment disputes under the Treaty. It can only be a dispute under the Treaty, if there is a clear violation of Treaty rights and obligations or a violation of contractual rights "of such a magnitude as to trigger the Treaty protection".[72] In their view, that was not the case here. The tribunal further opined that the connection between the Contract and the Treaty was the missing link here, and this is why a breach of contract could not be rendered susceptible to Treaty protection. It would have been different in other cases where that link was found to exist. However, that was certainly not the case here.[73]

The case of *Salini Construttori S.P.A. and Italstrade S.P.A. v The Hashemite Kingdom of Jordan*[74] concerned Article 2(4) of the Italy-Jordan BIT which stated that, "Each Contracting Party shall create and maintain in its territory a legal framework apt to guarantee to investors the continuity of legal treatment, including the compliance, in good faith, of all undertakings assumed with regard to each specific investor". The Tribunal held that Article 2(4) of the BIT did not represent a commitment on either Contracting Party to observe any obligation it had previously assumed, "with regards to specific investments of investors of the other contracting Party ..."[75] All the parties were committing to do in this instance is create and maintain a legal framework, which guaranteed the compliance of all undertakings it assumed with regard to each specific investor.[76]

The arbitral tribunal in *El Paso Energy International Company v Argentina*[77] adopted an equally narrow approach to the interpretation of umbrella clauses. The clause in question was contained in US-Argentina BIT, which provided that "each Party shall observe any obligation it may have entered into with regard to investments". El Paso thus argued that contractual breaches by the Argentine government would amount to a breach of the aforementioned BIT.

69 Paragraph 166.
70 Paragraph 168.
71 Award on Jurisdiction, ICSID Case No. ARB/03/11, 6 August 2004.
72 Paragraph 81.
73 Ibid.
74 Decision on Jurisdiction, ICSID Case No. ARB/02/13, 29 November 2004.
75 Paragraph 126.
76 Ibid.
77 Decision on Jurisdiction, ICSID Case No. ARB/03/15, 27 April 2006.

The Tribunal opined that it was necessary to distinguish between the State acting as a merchant and the State acting as a sovereign. Since the umbrella clause suggested that liability would arise out of commitments given by the State as a sovereign, it therefore means that coverage under the Treaty does not extend to breaches of an ordinary commercial contract entered into by the State or an entity owned by the State.[78] The tribunal thus distanced themselves from the wide interpretation given to umbrella clauses, and instead aligned itself with tribunals that had given them a much narrower interpretation. As such, they rejected El Paso's contention that a breach of contract on the part of the Argentine government should be considered as a breach of the BIT.

This narrow approach was followed in *Pan American Energy LLC and BP Argentina Exploration Company v Argentina*.[79] The tribunal in this case consisted of two of the same three arbitrators in the *El Paso* case. The Tribunal opined that:

> It would be strange indeed if the acceptance of a BIT entailed an international liability of the State going far beyond the obligation to respect the standards of protection of foreign investments embodied in the Treaty and rendered it liable for any violation of any commitment in national or international law 'with regard to investments'.[80]

In the case of *CMS Gas v Argentina*[81], the arbitral tribunal did find the government of Argentina internationally responsible, pursuant to the umbrella clause found in the US-Argentina BIT. However, such liability was restricted to contracts concluded between a host State, acting as a sovereign, and an investor. This in the tribunal's view, purely commercial aspects of a contract were not protected by a Treaty. However, protection is likely to be available in instances where government or public agencies interfere with the rights of an investor.[82]

It has thus been seen that there is a body of case law, under which the ICSID Tribunal displayed a reluctance to give a wide interpretation to umbrella clauses. The arguments propounded suggest that tribunals under this banner will not automatically determine that breach of a contract to which the State is a party renders the State liable under international law. Arbitral tribunals have also made a distinction between ordinary commercial contracts, under which the State is acting as a mere merchant and contracts fostering the process of foreign direct investment, under which the State is acting as a sovereign.

78 Paragraph 81.

79 *Pan American Energy LLC and BP Exploration Company v Argentina*, ICSID Case No. ARB/03/13 and *BP America Production Co. and Others v Argentina* ICSID Case No. ARB/04/8, Decision on Preliminary Objections, 27 July 2006.

80 Paragraph 110.

81 (2007) 14 ICSID Reports 251.

82 Ibid 299.

3.2.2.3 Contractual clauses

3.2.2.3.1 DISPUTE SETTLEMENT CLAUSE

One other means through which an investor may protect themselves from the consequences of the resource nationalism cycle is through the insertion of a dispute settlement clause. These are important to investors as they wish to ensure that any disputes arising will be heard by a neutral forum, rather than the national courts.[83] This arises out of a concern that the national courts may not be fully independent of the executive. For this reason, there is a possibility that national courts may render a decision against the investor, even where there is the existence of incontrovertible evidence. As such, investors will invariably insert a dispute resolution clause providing for mediation or arbitration. Mediation is a non-binding procedure under which a neutral third party, the mediator, assists the parties in arriving at their own decision.[84] This approach is advantageous as it brings the parties together. In the long run, it makes it easier for the parties to maintain long-term relationships with one another, after the dispute is brought to finality. The difficulty with this approach, however, is that it is non-binding, unless formalized through a Consent Order. Therefore, in the absence of a Consent Order from the Courts, the parties can easily depart from any solutions propounded during the mediation proceedings.

Parties can also resolve their disputes through arbitration. Under this process, a dispute is heard by an individual or panel of individuals referred to as the arbitral tribunal. The tribunal obtain their jurisdiction from the arbitration clause itself. The advantage of arbitration is that a decision rendered by the arbitral tribunal, which is referred to as an "arbitral award", is binding and enforceable. Once arbitral award has been rendered, the parties then seek recognition and enforcement. This is fostered through the Convention on the Recognition and Enforcement of Foreign Arbitral Awards (the New York Convention).[85]

Another advantage is that if the State unilaterally terminates a contract containing an arbitration clause, then the clause itself remains valid.[86] This owing to the principle of separability. Under this principle, the arbitration clause embedded in a contract is considered as separate from the main contract.[87] In the event that the contract elapses or is avoided, the arbitration clause itself remains valid. As such, a State cannot avoid being subjected to arbitration

83 Muthucumaraswamy Sornarajah, *The International Law on Foreign Investment* (3rd edn, CUP 2010) 286.

84 *World Intellectual Property Organization Guide to WIPO Mediation*, quoted in Tibor Várady, John J. Barceló and Arthur T. Von Mehren, *International Commercial Arbitration: A Transnational Perspective* (3rd edn, Thomson 2006) 2–3.

85 http://www.uncitral.org/uncitral/en/uncitral_texts/arbitration/NYConvention.html.

86 Janet A. Rosen, "Arbitration under Private International Law: The Doctrines of Separability and Compétence de la Compétence" (1993) 17 *Fordham International Law Journal* 599.

87 Ibid 606.

proceedings by simply terminating a concession agreement. As observed in *LIAMCO v Libya*[88]:

> It is widely accepted in international law and practice that an arbitration clause survives the unilateral termination by that State of the contract in which it is inserted and continues in force even after that termination. This is a logical consequence of the interpretation of the intention of the contracting parties, and appears to be one of the basic conditions for creating a favourable climate of foreign investment.[89]

Supplementing the arbitration clause is the choice-of-law clause. A choice of law clause or applicable law clause is a term inserted into the concession agreement. This clause stipulates that in the event that a dispute arises under a concession, then it is to be determined in accordance with the substantive law of a particular jurisdiction.[90] The insertion of this clause is a particularly sensitive issue.[91] This is owing to the fact that it involves two conflicting interests. On the one hand, the host State is interested in preserving and protecting its national sovereignty. On the other hand, it is in the investor's interest to choose a legal order that is stable and predictable.[92] The outcome depends largely upon the bargaining power of the parties. For example, the choice of law clause could refer exclusively to the law of the host State. Alternatively, the parties could select a law other than that of the host State. It could also be a combination of both.

3.2.2.3.2 STABILIZATION CLAUSES

Stabilization clauses are yet another means through which investors protect themselves from the consequences of the resource nationalism cycle. Under the obsolescing bargaining model, host State typically offer myriad incentives to the investor. However, these incentives are subject to subsequent alteration by the host State once the investment is sunk.[93] As a buffer against this, investors will insist on the insertion of stabilization clauses into the concession agreement. Under these clauses, the host State undertakes that it will not utilize its legislative and administrative prerogatives in a way that will have a detrimental effect on the investor. The inclusion of these clauses is not just a concern of the investor, other stakeholders such as lending institutions also insist on the insertion

88 *Libyan American Oil Company (LIAMCO) v Libya* (1981) 20 ILM 1.
89 Ibid 40.
90 See Christopher R. Drahozal, "Contracting Out of National Law: An Empirical Look at the New Law Merchant" (2005) 80 *Notre Dame Law Review* 523, 532–534.
91 Dolzer and Schreuer (n 4) 81.
92 Ibid.
93 See generally Vernon (n 18) and Brandon Marsh, "Preventing the Inevitable: The Benefits of Contractual Risk Engineering in the Light of Venezuela's Recent Oil Field Nationalization" (2008) 13 *Stanford Journal of Law Business & Finance* 453, 457.

of these clauses in the concession agreement.[94] Because lending institutions are the ones that finance projects, they are insistent on the insertion of stabilization clauses, as a form of insurance that they will get their money back from the investor, once they make a borrowing.

Stabilization clauses can also be supplemented by the insertion of renegotiation clauses. Renegotiation clauses are contractual mechanisms under which the parties are given the option of renewing, discussing and adapting the terms of a concession agreement.[95] Typically, these are activated upon the occurrence of a triggering event or during specific intervals.[96] The legal validity of these clauses is undisputed because they are inserted by the free will of the parties.[97] The distinction between renegotiation clauses and stabilization clauses is that the latter is concerned with the sanctity of contracts, whereas the former is concerned with maintaining the economic equilibrium.[98]

It has thus been seen from this section that resource nationalism is a cyclical phenomenon. During the advanced stages of the cycle, the natural resources of the host State experience a sustained upward trend, thus triggering in the host State a desire to maximize on the benefits accruing from its natural resource. In such circumstances, the host State either increases taxes or outrightly nationalizes assets belonging to the investor. As a buffer against this, investors seek to protect themselves in different ways. They, for example, can rely on investment insurance bodies such as MIGA. They may also rely on the protections contained in BITs and Multilateral Treaties. These include umbrella clauses. Moreover, they may rely on contractual clauses, such as arbitration clauses, choice-of-law clauses and renegotiation clauses. In addition to this, they may rely on stabilization clauses. The aim of the next section is to discuss these in depth.

3.3 Stabilization clauses

Clearly, the consequences of the resource nationalism cycle are a cause for concern when investing in a resource-rich nation. Thus, in order to insulate themselves, investors will often insist on the insertion of stabilization clauses into their concession agreements. Stabilization clauses are inserted in order to ensure that the agreement is not susceptible to future changes in the law.[99] This is accomplished by immunizing the concession agreement from the municipal law

94 Maniruzzaman (n 35) 95.

95 Sangwani Patrick Ng'ambi, *Resource Nationalism in International Investment Law* (Routledge 2016) 131.

96 See also John Y. Gotanda, "Renegotiation and Adaptation Clauses in International Contracts Revisited" (2003) 36 *Vanderbilt Journal of Transnational Law* 1461, 1462.

97 Abdullah Al Faruque, "Renegotiation and Adaptation of Petroleum Contracts: The Quest for Equilibrium and Stability" (2008) 9 *Journal of World Investment and Trade* 113, 129.

98 Dolzer and Schreuer (n 4) 85.

99 Christopher T. Curtis, "The Legal Security of Economic Development Agreements" (1988) 29 *Harvard International Law Journal* 317, 346.

of the host State and effectively internationalizing it.[100] As such, any future alterations in the law should, in the abstract, have no effect on a concession that contains a stabilization clause.[101] This section discusses the effect of stabilization clauses in concession agreements. It begins by looking at the types of stabilization clauses in existence. It then goes on to discuss the case law pertaining to stabilization clauses.

3.3.1 Types of stabilization clauses

There are different types of stabilization clauses: the stabilization clause *stricto sensu*, the intangibility clause and the economic stabilization clause. These are each discussed, in turn, in this subsection.

3.3.1.1 Stabilization clause stricto sensu

The first type is the "stabilization clause *stricto sensu*".[102] The purpose behind this clause is to ensure that the law existing at the time the concession was entered into will continue to subsist until it elapses.[103] The stabilization clause *stricto sensu* is thus worded in a way that it freezes the law of the host State, from the day that the contract is concluded, until it actually expires. An example of this clause is contained in the Concession Agreement of 1933, between Iran and the Anglo Iranian Oil Company. The aforementioned concession agreement provided that the "Concession shall not be annulled by the Government and the terms therein contained shall not be altered either by general or special legislation in the future, or by administrative measures or any other acts whatever of the executive authorities".[104] Thus, any legislative changes that are made by the host State will not in any way override the rights and obligations contained within the concession agreement.

Thus, in the event that there is a conflict between the provisions of the concession and any subsequent legislation, the former will supersede the latter.[105] This category also includes "tax stability clauses". The intention behind these is to ensure that the fiscal incentives that existed at the time that the concession were concluded remain intact until the end of the contract. Therefore, no new taxes

100 Abul F.M. Maniruzzaman, "Some Reflections on Stabilisation Techniques in International Petroleum, Gas and Mineral Agreements" (2005) 4 *International Energy Law and Taxation Review* 96, 97 and generally Arghyrios A. Fatouros, "International Law and the Internationalized Contract" (1980) 74 *American Journal of International Law* 134–141.

101 Bertrant Montembault, "The Stabilisation of State Contracts Using the Example of Oil Contracts: A Return of the Gods of Olympia" (2003) 6 *International Business Law Journal* 593, 599–601.

102 Curtis (n 99) 346.

103 Faruque (n 7) 319.

104 Esa Paasivirta, *Participation of States in International Contracts and Arbitral Settlement of Disputes* (Lakimiesluton Kustannus 1990) 162.

105 Faruque (n 7) 319.

introduced by the host government, during the tax stability period, can override the fiscal incentives contained within the concession.

3.3.1.2 Intangibility clause

The second type of stabilization clause is the "intangibility clause".[106] These clauses effectively stipulate that the concession cannot be altered or abrogated, except with the mutual consent of the parties.[107] Under the intangibility clause, the host State does not surrender any legislative or administrative prerogatives as such. However, much like the *stricto sensu* clauses, the purpose behind the intangibility clause is to prevent the State from unilaterally altering the terms of the agreement. This was certainly the clause utilized in the Production Sharing Contract of Indonesia between Pertamina and Overseas Petroleum Investment Corporation and Treasure Bay Enterprise Ltd.[108] It stated that "This contract shall not be annulled, amended or modified in any respect, except by mutual consent in writing of the parties hereto".[109]

3.3.1.3 Economic stabilization clause

Yet another type of stabilization clause is the "economic stabilization clause".[110] An example of this is the one contained in the agreement between the Republic of Gabon and Vanco Gabon Ltd. The aforementioned clause provided that:

> [T]he State guarantees to the Contractor, for the duration of the contract, the stability of the financial and economic conditions insofar as these conditions result from the Contract and from the regulations in force on the Effective Date.
>
> These obligations resulting from the Contract shall not be aggravated, and the general and overall equilibrium of the Contract shall not be affected in an important and lasting manner for the entire period of validity hereof. However, adjustments and modification of these provisions may be agreed upon by mutual consent.[111]

As such, the purpose behind this clause is to prohibit the State from passing any laws or taking any administrative action that makes the contract more expensive or onerous to perform. In the alternative, such a clause ensures that in instances where the government does pass such a law, then they would have to examine the adverse economic consequences of such action and restore the economic equilibrium.[112]

106 Curtis (n 99) 346.
107 Faruque (n 7) 319.
108 Article 17.2 of the Production Sharing Contract of Indonesia between Pertamina and Overseas Petroleum Investment Corp. and Treasure Bay Enterprise Ltd, quoted in Faruque (n 7) 319.
109 Ibid.
110 Faruque (n 7) 320.
111 Ibid.
112 Faruque (n 7) 320.

The precise effect of stabilization clauses has certainly been the subject of much academic debate.[113] Two schools of thought exist in this respect. The first school of thought is that stabilization clauses offer absolute protection to the investor.[114] This is owing to the fact that they circumvent any possibility of premature termination of the concession agreement through legislative means.[115] This argument is essentially grounded in the international law principle of *pacta sunt servanda*.[116] Under this principle, agreements freely entered into must be upheld.[117] On the other hand there are those who argue that stabilization clauses do not offer absolute protection to the investor.[118] There are doubts that a concession agreements can have the effect of preventing a host State from exercising its inalienable prerogatives.[119] One such example of this, is the State's right to nationalize.[120]

There is generally no consensus in the academic debate on this matter. However, it is clear from the case law that arbitral tribunals uphold the validity of stabilization clauses. This is on the basis of the principle of *pacta sunt servanda*. As such, all concession agreements containing stabilization clauses must be upheld.[121] The aim of this section is to examine the case law pertaining to stabilization clauses.

This section is divided into three subsections. Section 3.3.2.1 examines the early case law pertaining to stabilization clauses. These first cases, represented an early recognition that stabilization clauses were binding on the State. Section 3.3.2.2 examines the Libyan nationalization cases, namely: *BP v Libya*,[122] *Texaco v Libya*[123] and *LIAMCO v Libya*.[124] The particular significance of these cases is that they had a similar set of facts, and yet the three tribunals espoused different reasons for their outcomes. Finally, this section will look at the subsequent case law.

113 See Esa Paasirvirta, "Internationalization and Stabilization of Contracts Versus State Sovereignty" (1989) 60 *British Yearbook of International Law* 315, 316–323.

114 See Henry De Vries, "The Enforcement of Economic Development Agreements with Foreign States" (1984) 62 *University of Detroit Law Review* 1, 20–21; Margarita T.B. Coale, "Stabilisation Clauses in International Petroleum Transactions" (2002) 30 *Denver Journal of International Law and Policy* 217.

115 David Suratgar, "Considerations Affecting Choice of Law Clauses in Contracts between Governments and Foreign Nationals" (1962) 2 *Indian Journal of International Law* 273, 302.

116 *Blacks Law Dictionary* (8th edn, 2004) 1140.

117 Andreas F. Lowenfeld, "Lex Mercatoria: An Arbitrator's View" in Thomas E. Carbonneau (ed), *Lex Mercatoria and Arbitration* (Kluwer 1998) 89.

118 See Derek W. Bowett, "State Contracts with Aliens: Contemporary Developments on Compensation for Termination or Breach" (1988) 49 *British Yearbook of International Law* 49, 51–52.

119 Subrata K. Chatterjee, "The Stabilization Clause Myth in Investment Agreements" (1988) 5 *Journal of International Arbitration* 97, 110. See also *Oscar Chinn* (1934) PCIJ Series A/B No. 63, 23.

120 Piero Bernardini, "Stabilization and Adaptation in Oil and Gas Investments" (2008) 1 *Journal of World Energy Law and Business* 98, 101.

121 Peter Muchlinski, *Multinational Enterprises and the Law* (2nd edn, OUP 2007) 582.

122 (1979) 53 ILR 297.

123 (1978) 17 ILM 1.

124 (1977) ILR 141.

3.3.2 Case law on stabilization clauses

3.3.2.1 Earlier decisions on stabilization clauses

There are very few cases dealing with disputes between investors and host States, prior to the Second World War.[125] There are a number of reasons for this. The first is that the development of "cross-border subterranean resources" only began in earnest, at the end of the nineteenth century.[126] Second, there were also doubts as to whether private parties had the necessary *locus standi* to bring cases before an international tribunal. Moreover, international commercial arbitration and the infrastructure supporting it, was still in its infancy at the time.[127] Consequently, in instances where an investor was injured by the host State, action would traditionally be initiated by the home State of the investor, under the umbrella of diplomatic protection.[128]

One of the earliest cases dealing with stabilization clauses was that of *Lena Goldfields, Ltd. v. U.S.S.R.*[129] In this case, the Soviet Government had granted Lena Goldfields a concession to mine gold and other metals in the Urals and Siberia. Part of the concession was to run for fifty years, whilst the other part was to run for thirty-seven years. Lena Goldfields's operations commenced later in 1925. However, the Soviet government later created circumstances that rendered it impossible for Lena Goldfields to carry out its operations.[130] This was owing to a shift in government policy on capitalists in 1929.[131] Consequently, Lena Goldfields suffered great hostility and harassment, making it difficult for them to continue with their operations. When subsequent negotiations with the Soviet government collapsed, Lena Goldfields initiated arbitral proceedings against them.

One of the issues before the tribunal, was the effect of Article 76 of the concession. This contained a stabilization clause, under which the Soviet government had promised not to alter the agreement without the consent of Lena Goldfields. As such, this clause was to insulate Lena Goldfields from any future legislative or administrative action taken by the Soviet government, to override the contractual rights in the concession.

125 Jason W. Yackee, "*Pacta Sunt Servanda* and State Promises to Foreign Investors before Bilateral Investment Treaties: Myth and Reality" (2009) 32 *Fordham International Law Journal* 1550, 1572.

126 Nakagawa (n 6) 2.

127 Ibid.

128 Edwin M. Borehand, "Contractual Claims in International Law" (1913) 13 *Columbia Law Review* 457, 457.

129 Arthur Nussbaum, "The Arbitration between the Lena Goldfields, Ltd. and the Soviet Government" (1950–51) *Cornell Law Quarterly* 31, 42. This is a reproduction of the award, as the original got lost.

130 Christoph H. Schreuer, "Unjustified Enrichment in International Law" (1974) 22 *American Journal of Comparative Law* 281–301, 288.

131 See V.V. Vedeer, "The Lena Goldfields Arbitration: the Historical Roots of the Three Ideas" (1998) 47 *International and Comparative Law Quarterly* 747, 761.

The Court of Arbitration took the view that the concession between Lena Goldfields and the Soviet government had been "internationalized". As such, the general principles of law may be applied in protecting the contractual interests of private entities like Lena Goldfields.[132] By repudiating the contract, the Soviet government had unjustly enriched itself. Therefore, Lena Goldfields was awarded a sum of $65 million. This included lost future profits.[133] Although the arbitral tribunal did not elaborate further on the stabilization clause itself, this case represents one of the earliest recognitions that something other than the national law of the host State governs concession agreements.[134]

Subsequent decisions have generally followed the position of the tribunal in *Lena Goldfields*. This is reflected in the case of *Sapphire International Petroleum Ltd. v. National Iranian Oil Co. (NIOC).*[135] This case concerned the NIOC and Sapphire Petroleum Ltd, a Canadian company, who entered into a contract in June 1958. The purpose of the contract was to expand the production and exportation of Iranian oil. Sapphire had to provide the technical know-how, financial muscle and the organization necessary to fulfil the obligations stipulated in the contract. In addition, it was under an obligation to make a minimum investment of $8 million in four years. There was a stabilization clause in the agreement which read as follows:

> No general or statutory enactment, no administrative measure or decree of any kind, made either by the government or by any governmental authority in Iran (central or local), including NIOC, can cancel the agreement or affect or change its provisions, or prevent or hinder its performance. No cancellation, amendment or modification can take place except with the agreement of the two parties.[136]

In order to carry out their obligations, the parties set up the Iranian Canada Oil Company (ICRAN). ICRAN was a "joint stock company and non-profit corporation" which was to carry out the operations under the contract on behalf of Sapphire and NIOC. However, when it came to prospecting, ICRAN would act only as Sapphire's agent. Both parties each subscribed to half the share capital of ICRAN. This would cost each party $5,000.

In August of 1958, Sapphire Petroleums Ltd, assigned its rights and obligations under the contract to Sapphire International Petroleums Ltd (Sapphire International). Sapphire International was wholly owned by Sapphire Petroleums Ltd.

132 Ibid 30, paragraph 22.
133 Yackee (n 125) 1575.
134 Coale (n 114) 227, See also "In the Matter of an Arbitration Between Petroleum Development (Trucial Coast) Ltd and the Sheikh of Abu Dhabi" (1952) 1 *International and Comparative Law Quarterly* 247, 260 and *Ruler of Qatar v International Marine Oil Company Ltd* (1953) 20 ILR 534.
135 (1967) 35 ILR 136.
136 Ibid 140.

Sapphire Petroleums Ltd paid NIOC a sum of $3,500 for the registration of Sapphire and Sapphire International in Tehran.

The contract itself was divided into two periods. The first period was to be a prospecting period and the second was to be an extraction and sale period. During the prospecting period, all expenses were to be reimbursed to Sapphire, through ICRAN, on the basis of accounts submitted by Sapphire. Once the extraction and sale period commenced, both parties were to jointly cover all expenses arising.

According to the contract, the first period would commence six months after the start date of the contract. Drilling on the other hand was to commence two years after the start date of the contract. In addition to this, the contract stated that if Sapphire failed to carry out its obligations within the stipulated timeframes, then NIOC would have the right to cancel the contract six months after the expiration of the aforementioned period. In that event, Sapphire would be liable to pay NIOC an indemnity of $350,000, except in the case of force majeure. This payment was guaranteed in a form of a bank guarantee, which was provided to NIOC.

Sapphire International commenced work in the designated concession area. In May 1959, they sent two reports on the expenses incurred from the date of the contract until 31 March 1959. Expenses incurred up to that point amounted to $302,545.25. NIOC refused to refund these expenses. NIOC contended that it had not been consulted prior to the commencement of operations, which was required under the contract.

In July 1959, Sapphire International wrote a letter to the Shah of Iran, requesting a refund of their losses. The Prime Minister of Iran replied on 5 September 1959. In this reply, the Prime Minister stated that Sapphire International had not fulfilled its obligations. As such, NIOC were under no obligation to release the refund. He thus referred Sapphire International back to NIOC for the settlement of the dispute.

Given this background, and the ensuing dispute with NIOC, Sapphire International decided not to risk signing a drilling contract with NIOC. On 24 July 1960, NIOC wrote to Sapphire Informing them that they had not yet commenced with their drilling operations. Six months later, on 24 January 1961, NIOC cancelled the contract and proceeded to cash the $350,000 indemnity provided by Sapphire International. This was despite formal opposition by Sapphire International. Pursuant to Article 41 of the Contract, Sapphire International initiated arbitral proceedings against NIOC. Because NIOC failed to appoint an arbitrator, a sole arbitrator was thus appointed by the Swiss Federal Court.

In this case, the arbitrator fund that the premature termination of the Contract imposed a duty on the State to compensate Sapphire International. This was owing to the principle of *pacta sunt servanda*, which prescribes that contractual undertakings must be respected. He accordingly rendered an award in favour of Sapphire International. As far as the arbitrator was concerned, NIOC's deliberate failure to fulfil its contractual obligations, amounted to a breach of contract.[137]

137 Ibid 181.

From the preceding cases, it can be seen that arbitral tribunals are inclined to render an award in favour of the complainant investor, in the event that the host State prematurely terminates a contract. Thus, once a State enters into a contract, it cannot unilaterally abrogate its terms. Doing so amounts to a breach of contract.

However, this position has certainly been challenged in later cases. This is owing to the fact that precluding the State from utilizing its prerogatives through contractual means, would be incongruous with the doctrine of permanent sovereignty over natural resources. Although arbitral tribunals have given due consideration to this contention, it is not one that is looked upon with a kindly eye.[138] For example, in *Saudi Arabia v. Arabian American Oil Co. (Aramco)*[139] the government of Saudi Arabia contended that the stabilization clause contained within the concession, was not binding upon the State. In their view, to hold otherwise would militate against Saudi Arabia's sovereignty. The arbitral tribunal rejected this argument and contended that:

> [b]y reason of its very sovereignty within its territorial domain, the State possess the legal powers to grant rights [by] which it forbids itself to withdraw before the end of the concession, with the reservation of the Clauses of the Concession Agreement relating to its revocation. Nothing can prevent a State, in the exercise of its sovereignty, from binding itself irrevocably by the provisions of a concession and from granting to the concessionaire irretractable rights. Such rights have the character of acquired rights.[140]

The arbitral tribunal thus opined that a State use "sovereignty" as the basis for going back on its decision to enter into a concession agreement, once it has renounced the right to exercise some of its sovereign prerogatives. This is owing to the fact that once the State has accepted a stabilization clause, it creates a "legitimate expectation" in the mind of the investor.[141] Once the State does so, it cannot go back on it. The arbitral tribunal thus rejected the sovereignty argument. The *Aramco* case thus suggests that, as a general rule, sovereignty cannot excuse the host State from fulfilling its contractual obligations.

From the earlier cases, it has been seen that arbitral tribunals endorsed the view that stabilization clauses give absolute protection to foreign investors. Although the sovereignty argument has been raised, this has generally been rejected by arbitral tribunals. This is owing to the fact that entering into these contracts is a

138 Sangwani Ng'ambi, "Stabilisation Clauses and the Zambian Windfall Tax" (2010) 1 *Zambia Social Science Journal* 107–117, 109.

139 (1963) 27 ILR 117.

140 Ibid 168.

141 Prosper Weil, "Les clauses de stabilization ou d'intangibilité insérées dans les accords de development économique" in *Mélangues offerts à Charles Rousseau* (A Pedone 1974) 326, See also Martti Koskemeni, "What Use for Sovereignty Today" (2011) 1 *Asian Journal of International Law*, 61–70, 62 who says, "They had been able to bind themselves because they were sovereigns. If they were not able to bind themselves- and thus receive the benefits they were looking for – well, then they could not really be sovereigns, could they?"

facet of sovereignty. Such sovereignty is surrendered once. States bind themselves to an agreement with a foreign investor. This is a trend that continues with the later cases, which is the topic of the next subsection.

3.3.2.2 Later cases

3.3.2.2.1 THE LIBYAN NATIONALIZATION CASES

The Libyan nationalization cases arose after the government of Libya nationalized foreign-owned companies. The three cases covered here are *BP v Libya*,[142] *Texaco Overseas Oil Petroleum Co./California Asiatic Oil Co. v Libya*[143] and *LIAMCO v Libya*.[144] The facts are that Libya became an independent State in 1951. At the time Libya was impoverished and had very few known natural resources. As such, much of Libya's population was sparse and uneducated. Furthermore, 90% of the country consisted of desert land. As a result of this, Libya only possessed a very small amount of arable land. Libya had very bleak economic prospects, upon attaining her independence.[145]

However, between 1951 and 1979, Libya discovered vast oil reserves. Consequently, by 1979, Libya's income was estimated to have exceeded $16 billion dollars from oil exports. Libya thus went from being an impoverished country to being ranked among the world's top fifteen richest nations. Earning $6,680 per capita, Libya was also the highest earner in Africa.[146]

In order to explore and exploit their vast oil reserves, the government of Libya had to rely heavily on the inflow of foreign direct investment.[147] To facilitate this process, the government of Libya introduced the Libyan Petroleum Law of 1955, which outlined the legal mechanisms under which oil concessions were to be granted. The standard deed of concessions, according to Article 9, was to be utilized when granting all concessions in Libya.

Three key provisions were included within the standard concession agreements. These were the stabilization clause, the arbitration clause and the choice of law clause. The stabilization clause was contained in Clause 16 of the standard concession. It provided that:

> 1 The Government of Libya, the Commission and the appropriate provincial authorities will take all steps necessary to ensure that the Company enjoys all the rights conferred by this Concession. The contractual rights expressly created by this Concession shall not be altered except by mutual consent of the parties.

142 (n 122).
143 (n 123).
144 (n 124).
145 For a more elaborate socio-economic background see Robert B. Von Mehren and P. Nicholas Kourides, "International Arbitration between States and Foreign Private Parties: The Libyan Nationalization Cases" (1981) 75 *American Journal of International Law* 476, 477–479.
146 The World Bank, *World Development Report of 1979*.
147 Von Mehren and Kourides (n 145) 477.

2 This Concession shall throughout the period of its validity be construed in accordance with the Petroleum Law and the Regulations in force on the date of execution of the Agreement of Amendment by which this paragraph (2) was incorporated into this Concession Agreement. Any amendment to or repeal of such Regulations shall not affect the contractual rights of the Company without its consent.[148]

Clause 28(1) of the standard concession contained the arbitration clause. All parties were thus to settle all disputes by arbitration, rather than the national forums. If a dispute arose, then it was to be referred to an arbitral tribunal. The tribunal was to consist of two arbitrators and an Umpire. The investor and the government of Libya were each to appoint one arbitrator. Those two appointed arbitrators would then select a third arbitrator, who would be the Umpire. As per the clause, the party initiating the arbitral proceedings was required to make a written request to the other party, specifying the nature of the dispute and informing them of the name of the arbitrator they had selected.[149] The other party was then to appoint their own arbitrator in ninety days. If the other party failed to do so within the stipulated timeframe, then the Vice President of the International Court of Justice would have to appoint a Sole Arbitrator.[150]

There was also a choice of law clause, which was contained in Clause 28(7) of the standard concession. The original choice of law clause provided that, "This Concession shall be governed by and interpreted in accordance with the Laws of Libya and such principles and rules of international law as may be relevant, and the umpire or sole arbitrator shall base his award upon those laws, principles and rules". Subsequent alterations to this meant that only the principles of Libyan law, that were common with those of international law, would be applied in the governance and interpretation of the concession. In the absence of such principles, the general principles of law would be applicable, including those applied by international tribunals.[151] These changes were effected to ensure that more equitable treatment would be afforded to foreign oil companies operating in Libya.

In 1969, Colonel Muammar Gaddafi overthrew the government of Libya, in a bloodless coup. Colonel Gaddafi thus became Chairman of the Revolutionary Command Council of Libya. In December 1971, the Libyan government nationalized all assets belonging to British Petroleum in the Hunt/BP concession, through Decree No. 115.[152] This was ostensibly in retaliation to the fact that Britain did nothing to stop Iran from invading the islands of Abu Musa and the Greater and Lesser Tumb in November 1971. The islands were still nominally under British protection through a Treaty, which was due to expire the day after

148 (n 122) 322.

149 Clause 28(2).

150 Clause 28(3), See also Tibor Várady, John J. Barceló and Arthur T. Von Mehren, *International Commercial Arbitration: A Transnational Perspective* (3rd edn, Thomson 2006) 114–115.

151 Amendments to the Petroleum Law, Libyan Rev., January 1966, at 26, 27.

152 Libya: Law on the Nationalization of the British Petroleum Exploration Company (1972) 11 ILM 380.

Iran invaded these islands. Britain did consequently receive much condemnation from the Arab world.

Early in 1973, Libya nationalized all of Bunker Hunt's interest in the Hunt/BP deed of concession. They cited America's support for Israel in the Arab-Israeli conflict, as the basis of this nationalization. In the same year, through decree No. 66 of 1973, they also nationalized 51% of assets belonging to TOPCO, CLASIATIC and LIAMCO.[153] In 1974, they nationalized the remaining 49% of assets belonging to the aforementioned companies, through Decree No. 10[154] and Decree No. 11 of 1974.[155]

The parties, namely BP, TOPCO/CLASIATIC and LIAMCO, thus initiated arbitral proceedings against the government of Libya. In all three cases, the parties had written to the government of Libya, indicating that they had appointed their arbitrator. The government of Libya initially refused to participate in the proceedings. Therefore, in all three cases, Sole Arbitrators were appointed by the Vice-President of the International Court of Justice, pursuant to Clause 28(3) of the concession agreement.

In all three cases, the efficacy of the stabilization clauses in relation to the nationalizations was raised. In *BP v Libya*[156] the arbitrator held that the Libyan government's nationalization of BP's assets was illegal. However, it would seem that the arbitrator arrived at this decision on the basis that the taking was confiscatory, rather than on the fact that there was a stabilization clause in the concession. The tribunal focussed on the fact that had been two years since the nationalization had taken place, and yet BP had still not received compensation.[157]

The arbitrator in *BP v Libya* said very little about the actual stabilization clause. In determining whether the Libyan government was liable for breach of contract, the arbitrator looked instead at the choice of law clause. Under this clause, the applicable law was *inter alia* the "general principles of law".[158] It was clear that there had been a breach of contract and that BP was entitled to damages.[159] The arbitrator opined that the rules dealing with repudiation of an agreement were "too elementary and voluminous" to require any further elaboration.[160]

153 See Libya: Law on Nationalization of Oil Companies Legislation and Regulations (1974) 13 ILM 60, other concession holders that were affected by this decree were: Esso Standard of Libya Inc., Grace Petroleum Corp., Esso Sirte Co., Inc., Shell Exploratie En Productie Maatschappij, Mobil Oil of Libya Inc., and Gelsenberg A.G. (Libya). There were some corporations that were not affected by this and these were Aquitaine Libye and Elf-Libye which were French and Hispanica de Petrolos which was a Spanish corporation.

154 Von Mehren and Kourides (n 145) 485.

155 Bernard Taverne, *Petroleum, Industry and Governments: A Global Study of the Involvement of Industry and Government in the Production and Use of Petroleum* (2nd edn, Kluwer 2008) 197.

156 (n 122).

157 Ibid 329.

158 Ibid 303.

159 Ibid 357.

160 Ibid 329.

The arbitrator in *Texaco Overseas Oil Petroleum Co./California Asiatic Oil Co. v Libya*[161] was much more elaborate in arriving at his decision. In this case, the Libyan government contended that upholding the stabilization clause militated against the principle of permanent sovereignty over natural resources. The arbitrator disagreed with this contention. This was owing to the fact that under the principle of *pacta sunt servanda*, it was in fact possible for a sovereign to bind itself to contract with a foreign investor. The choice of law clause contained in Clause 28(7) of the concession stipulated that, *inter alia*, Libyan law would be applicable. Sharia Law is a source of Libyan law and it provides that once parties have entered into a contract, they are bound by it. In fact, under Sharia law, a higher standard is applied to the sovereign or government than it would to private parties, because the sovereign has great discretionary powers at its disposal. Therefore, in order to set an example to his or her subjects, the sovereign is held to greater standard than that which would be applied to its citizens. This rule equally applies to agreements entered into with non-Muslims.[162]

The arbitrator also looked at the General Assembly Resolution 1803 and the Charter on the Economic Rights and Duties of States. He found that General Assembly Resolution 1803 certainly endorsed the view that foreign investment agreements are to be observed in good faith.[163] Although the arbitrator rejected the binding force of the Charter on the Economic Rights and Duties of States,[164] he did observe that it also explicitly provided that "international obligations" are to be fulfilled "in good faith".[165]

Furthermore, the arbitrator held that the stabilization clause did not impinge upon the Libya's sovereign prerogatives. This was owing to the fact that Libya's sovereign powers remained intact and could still be exercised against persons with whom they had not entered into a concession agreement with. In the arbitrator's view, "a State cannot invoke its sovereignty to disregard commitments freely undertaken through the exercise of this same sovereignty, and cannot through measures belonging to its internal order make null and void the rights of the contracting party which has performed its various obligations under the contract".[166] Thus, contracts entered into between the investor and the host State must be respected, otherwise it would undermine the credibility of States. It would also create an imbalance between the parties, because creating a system where investors are bound by the terms of the agreement whilst States are not. This would have an adverse effect on the principle of good faith. As such, the conception that States are not bound by stabilization clauses by virtue of their sovereignty was vehemently rejected.[167] As such, the principle of permanent

161 (n 123).
162 Ibid 23, paragraph 65.
163 Ibid 24, paragraph 68.
164 Ibid 30, paragraph 88.
165 Ibid 31, paragraph 90.
166 Ibid 23–24, paragraphs 65–68.
167 Ibid 31, paragraph 91.

sovereignty over natural resources does not generally excuse the host State from upholding its contractual obligations.

The decision in the preceding case can be contrasted with that in *LIAMCO v Libya*.[168] The arbitral tribunal in this case opined that stabilization clauses do not affect the State's sovereign right to expropriate property belonging to foreign investors. Holding otherwise would amount to an intolerable interference with the State's right to permanent sovereignty over natural resources.

On the one hand, it would thus appear that arbitral tribunals may positively respond to the sovereignty argument.[169] However, to argue that the *LIAMCO* award renders the principle of *pacta sunt servanda* obsolete is questionable.[170] This is owing to the fact that the arbitrator's position on sovereignty pertained only to the issue of damages. The arbitrator in this case was deciding upon whether to apply the "Hull Principle", under which adequate compensation would then be payable. This would have included lost future profits in the compensation award.

The arbitrator doubted the applicability of the Hull Principle under customary international law. The Arbitrator opined that the inclusion of lost future profits in the compensation award was a controversial one.[171] Because the nationalization was lawful, in the sense that it was non-discriminatory and for a public purpose, any determination of future profits had to be considered in terms of "equity" rather than "adequacy". Moreover, the arbitrator acknowledged that the contract could not be validly terminated without the "mutual consent of the contracting parties, in compliance with the said principle of the sanctity of contracts and particularly with the explicit terms of Clause 16 of the Agreements".[172] For these reasons, it is difficult to argue that this case represented a rejection of stabilization clauses in favour of sovereignty.[173]

From the Libyan decisions, it has been seen that although they all had the same facts, the arbitral tribunals arrived at entirely different reasons for their outcomes. The *BP* and *Texaco* cases seem to suggest that stabilization clauses afford absolute protection to investors. *LIAMCO* takes a more moderate stance. It does not absolutely reject the sovereignty argument but rather takes it into account when determining the amount of compensation payable. In this respect, the sanctity of contracts was still respected by the *LIAMCO* tribunal. However, it was not implemented in a way that punishes the host State from exercising its right to nationalize, even where the concession contains a stabilization clause.

168 (n 124) 141.
169 Ng'ambi (n 138) 111.
170 Yackee (n 125) 1589, although cf. Andrew Guzman, "Why LDCs Sign Treaties That Hurt Them: Explaining the Popularity of Bilateral Investment Treaties" (1998) 38 *Virginia Journal of International Law* 639.
171 *LIAMCO v Libya* (n 124) 131–132.
172 Ibid 62.
173 Yackee (n 125) 1590.

3.3.2.2.2 AWARDS AFTER THE LIBYAN NATIONALIZATION CASES

Subsequent cases have also generally supported the sanctity of contracts when it comes to the applicability of stabilization clauses.[174] In *Revere Copper & Brass Inc. v Overseas Private Investment Corporation*,[175] where Revere Jamaica Alumna, a subsidiary of Revere Copper & Brass, had constructed and was operating a bauxite mining plant in Jamaica. Their 1967 agreement with the Jamaican government provided for tax stability. However, when a new government was elected seven years later, they proceeded to significantly raise taxes, in contravention to the 1967 agreement. Revere was adversely affected and shut down its plant.

The Overseas Private Investment Corporation (OPIC), rejected Revere Copper's expropriation claim, on the basis that Jamaica had not actually taken away Revere's licence or physical assets. Revere Copper thus initiated arbitration proceedings against OPIC.

The arbitral tribunal opined that the government of Jamaica had attracted long-term foreign direct investment by *inter alia*, affording tax breaks and other assurances for limited periods of time.[176] According to the arbitral tribunal, the State can certainly impose limits on its sovereign powers when they enter into agreements with investors. This is in a similar fashion to when they issue long-term government bonds on foreign markets. In the tribunal's view:

> Under international law the commitments made in favour of foreign nationals are binding notwithstanding the power of Parliament and other governmental organs under the domestic Constitution to override or nullify such commitments Any other position would mean in this case that Jamaica could not in the exercise of its sovereign powers obtain foreign private capital to develop its resources or attract foreign industries. To suggest that for the purposes of obtaining foreign private capital the Government could only issue contracts that were non-binding would be meaningless. As the contracts were made in the sense that the commitments were set out in unqualified legal form, international law will give effect to them. For the purposes of this proceeding they must be regarded as binding.[177]

The sovereignty argument was raised again in the case of *AGIP v. Popular Republic of Congo*.[178] The tribunal rejected sovereignty argument and held that the stabilization clause in the agreement between the State of Congo and AGIP was binding. The facts of the case were that the government of Congo had

174 But cf. Dolzer and Schreuer (n 4) 82–85.
175 (1978) 17 ILM 1321.
176 Ibid.
177 Ibid.
178 (1982) 21 ILM 726.

nationalized the nation's oil distribution sector in 1974. AGIP was the only company that remained unaffected by these nationalizations. AGIP had entered into an agreement for the sale of 50% of their shares, to the government of Congo. This agreement contained several stabilization clauses. Congo nationalized the company by decree. Consequently, there were questions as to whether the said nationalization was compatible with the stabilization clauses in the agreement between Congo and AGIP. On the sovereignty argument the tribunal opined that:

> These stabilization clauses, which were freely entered into by the Government, do not affect the principle of its legislative and regulatory sovereignty since it retains both with respect to those, whether nationals or foreigners, with whom the Government has not entered into such undertakings, and that, in the present case, they are limited to rendering the modifications to the legislative regulatory provisions provided for in the Agreement, unopposable to the other contracting party.[179]

As such, the arbitral tribunal held that the stabilization clauses contained with the agreement concerned were freely entered into and accepted by the government of Congo. The State still retained its legislative and regulatory powers, they just could not be applied against AGIP or any other investor with whom they had an agreement.[180] As such, the Government of Congo was under an international obligation to compensate AGIP for any damage suffered as a result of the nationalization.[181]

The sovereignty argument was also rejected in the subsequent case of *Aminoil v Kuwait*.[182] The facts of this case are that in 1948, the Ruler of Kuwait had granted the American Independent Oil Company (AMINOIL) a sixty-year concession to explore and exploit Kuwait's oil and gas reserves. These were located in Kuwait's hold of the neutral zone between itself and Saudi Arabia. At the time that the agreement was signed, Kuwait was still a British Protectorate. The concession contained a stabilization clause, which read as follows:

> The Shaikh shall not by general or special legislation or by administrative measures or by any other act whatever annuls this Agreement except as provided in Article 11. No alteration shall be made in terms of this Agreement by either the Shaikh or the Company except in the event of the Shaikh and the Company jointly agreeing that it is desirable in the interests of both parties to make certain alterations, deletions or additions to this Agreement.[183]

179 Paragraphs 86–88.
180 Ibid 735, paragraph 86.
181 Ibid, paragraphs 86–88.
182 (1982) 21 ILM 976.
183 Ibid 990–991.

Kuwait obtained its independence from Britain on 19 June 1961 and proceeded to amend the 1948 concession.[184] Their aim was to conform with the fifty-fifty profit sharing model, which had now become commonplace in the Middle East.[185] When OPEC became a more influential force throughout the Middle East, pressure mounted on AMINOIL to agree to greater government participation. This included the imposition of higher taxes by the Kuwaiti government. AMINOIL agreed to these changes.[186]

After the October War of 1973, oil prices quadrupled, thereby increasing AMINOIL's profits. This was despite the fact that the government had already increased taxes and royalty rates. Negotiations thus continued and the new agreement was proposed by AMINOIL. Under this agreement, AMINOIL's profits would amount to seventy cents per barrel, or $18–20 million per year. The government, on the other hand, proposed a plan under which AMINOIL would gain substantially lower profits of twenty-five cents per barrel. This essentially translated to $7.5 million per year.[187]

Despite continuing negotiations, the government of Kuwait proceeded to nationalize AMINOIL, through Decree No. 124.[188] As such, the concession was terminated and all property belonging to AMINOIL reverted to the State.[189] Article 3 established a Compensation Committee, whose task was "to assess the fair compensation due to the Company as well as the Company's outstanding obligations to the State or other parties".[190] Thereafter, the State was to "pay what the Committee decides within one month of being notified of the Committee's decision".[191] AMINOIL refused to appear before this committee. It instead initiated arbitral proceedings in London, pursuant to the 1948 agreement.

One of the fundamental questions raised during the arbitral proceedings was whether the stabilization clause contained in the nationalization decree was unlawful. In the arbitral tribunals opinion, "a straightforward and direct reading of [the stabilization clause] can lead to the conclusion that they prohibit any nationalization".[192] However, the tribunal ultimately held that the stabilization clause did not preclude the government of Kuwait from nationalizing assets belonging to Aminoil.

Counsel for the government of Kuwait argued *inter alia* that giving effect to the stabilization clause would adversely affect the State's right to permanent sovereignty over natural resources.[193] Although the arbitral tribunal rejected this argument, they did acknowledge that the stabilization clause here could only

184 Ibid 991.
185 See Andreas Lowenfeld, *International Economic Law* (2nd edn, OUP 2008) 503.
186 Ibid.
187 Ibid.
188 (n 182) 998, paragraph 29.
189 Ibid.
190 Ibid.
191 Ibid.
192 Ibid 1020, paragraph 88.
193 Ibid 1021, paragraph 90.

be effective, if the government of Kuwait had expressly stipulated that it would not nationalize AMINOIL's assets, during the stability period. The tribunal noted that it is possible for the State to limit its right to nationalize. However, they would have to explicitly say so in the concession agreement.[194] Furthermore, such a clause would only be applicable for a relatively limited period.[195] In this case the clause ran for a period of sixty years, which in the estimation of the arbitral tribunal was "especially long".[196] It can be inferred from this decision that stabilization clauses only preclude a host State from nationalizing they expressly say they will not and if the clause is only applicable for a limited timeframe. It is not quite clear what amounts to a limited timeframe.

From these cases, it can be seen that as a general rule, arbitral tribunals support the sanctity of contracts and accordingly uphold stabilization clauses.[197] Even in moderate cases like *LIAMCO* and *Aminoil*, it can be seen that tribunals do not attack the efficacy of stabilization clauses *per se*. In the former case, the nationalization was still a "source of liability to compensate the concessionaire".[198] In the latter case, the stabilization clause would ordinarily have been rendered valid, had it been more specific and ran for a reasonable period. As such, it can be seen that as a general rule, states are bound to uphold concessions for the entirety of the stability period. If the State unilaterally terminates a concession, then it will have to pay compensation to the investor.

3.4 Conclusion

It could thus be concluded that the major concern of foreign investors is the stability of the concession agreement, once the investment has been sunk and operations have commenced. This is owing to the fact that the State may utilize its administrative and legislative prerogatives, in a way that adversely affects the investor. In order to avert this, investors will often insist on the insertion of stabilization clauses in the concession agreement.

194 cf. *Amoco International Finance Corp. v Government of the Islamic Republic of Iran* (1987) 15 Iran-US CT Rep 189.

195 Ibid 1022, paragraph 91.

196 (n 182) 1023, paragraph 95.

197 See the later case *Company Z (Republic of Xanadu) v State Organization ABC (Republic of Utopia)* (1983) 8 Y.B. Comm Arb 94. See also *Parkerings-Compagniet v Lithuania, Award*, 11 September 2007, ICSID Case No. ARB/05/8, where the tribunal opined at para 332 that, "It is each State's undeniable right and privilege to exercise its sovereign legislative power. A State has the right to enact, modify or cancel a law at its own discretion. Save for the existence of an agreement, in the form of a stabilization clause or otherwise, there is nothing objectionable about the amendment brought to the regulatory framework existing at the time an investor made its investment. As a matter of fact, any businessman or investor knows that law will evolve over time. What is prohibited however is for a State to act unfairly, unreasonably or inequitably in the exercise of its legislative power".

198 Ibid 60.

Stabilization clauses are an undertaking on the part of the host State that it will not use its administrative or legislative prerogatives in a manner that has a material adverse on the investment. The clause effectively freezes the law of the host State or at least ensures that no unilateral changes may be made to the concession, without the mutual consent of both parties. In essence, these clauses are designed to ensure that the concession agreement subsists for the timeframe stipulated therein. Furthermore, they act as a buffer against the advanced stages of the resource nationalism cycle, where states seek to maximize the benefits accruing from high mineral prices. This is either accomplished through increasing taxes or outright nationalization of the investors assets.

The case law pertaining to stabilization clauses seems to suggest that arbitral tribunals uphold the validity of stabilization clauses. Although there have been contentions that stabilization clauses militate against the principle of permanent sovereignty over natural resources, arbitral tribunals have generally rejected them. This is owing to the fact that entering into agreements in the first place is a facet of sovereignty. Thus, States cannot use sovereignty as an excuse for failing to uphold their contractual obligations. This is particularly the case because stabilization clauses elicit a legitimate expectation on the part of the investor. As such, stabilization clauses are upheld and respected by arbitral tribunals.

The difficulty with this position however is that it leads to rigidity in the contractual regime governing the relationship between the host State and the investor. One of the major concerns is the effect that stabilization clauses have on the State's ability to implement new human rights legislation at a domestic level. The passage of new human rights legislation in the host State means new obligations for the investor. These new obligations may have pecuniary consequences on the investor, in which case the State would have compensate the former. The monetary consequences of developing national human rights may deter a host State from doing so. The purpose of the next chapter is to discuss the effect that the stabilization clauses have on the host State's ability to pass new human rights legislation.

4 Stabilization clauses and human rights concerns

4.1 Introduction

From the preceding chapter, it has been seen that stabilization clauses aim to insulate the investor from non-commercial risks associated with foreign direct investment.[1] This is accomplished through a commitment on the part of the host State that they will not undertake any legislative or administrative actions that have an adverse impact on the investor.[2] In the event that the host State does unilaterally abrogate the concession agreement, through legislative or administrative means, there is a duty to pay compensation.[3]

There are two standards of compensation under international investment law. These are the Hull Principle and the appropriate compensation standard.[4] Under the former, compensation payable is to be prompt, adequate and effective.[5] The "adequacy" of the compensation is contingent not only on restoring the investor's sunk costs but also on the inclusion of lost future profits.[6] Under the appropriate compensation standards, the amount payable is determined on a case-by-case basis. However, arbitral tribunals will invariably include lost future profits in the compensation award, on the basis of the investor's legitimate expectations.

1 Lorenzo Cotula, "Reconciling Regulatory Stability and Evolution of Environmental Standards in Investment Contracts: Towards a Rethink of Stabilization Clauses" (2008) 1 *Journal of World Energy Law & Business* 158, 159.

2 Ibid.

3 Edith Penrose, George Joffé and Paul Stevens, "Nationalisation of Foreign-owned Property for a Public Purpose: An Economic Perspective on Appropriate Compensation" (1992) 55 *Modern law Review* 351, 352.

4 Sangwani Patrick Ng'ambi, "Permanent Sovereignty over Natural Resources and the Sanctity of Contracts: From the Angle of *Lucrum Cessans*" (2015) 12 *Loyola University Chicago International Law Review* 153, 165.

5 See Frank G. Dawson and Burns H. Weston, "'Prompt, Adequate and Effective': A Universal Standard of Compensation" (1962) 30 *Fordham Law Review* 727.

6 See *AGIP v Congo* (1982) 21 ILM 726 and Richard J. Smith, "The United States Government Perspective on Expropriation and Investment in Developing Countries" (1976) 9 *Vanderbilt Journal of Transnational Law* 517, 519.

Whilst stabilization clauses protect the investor's legitimate expectations, they may serve to prevent the State from exercising its legitimate public functions. One of these functions is upholding both national and international human rights standards. The difficulty arises when the host State seeks to pass new legislation in order to improve human rights standards within their jurisdiction.[7] New human rights legislation may mean increased obligations on the part of the investor. Consequently, the host State could face a heavy claim for compensation from the investor. The prospect of having to indemnify an investor every single time the host State wishes to enhance its human rights ultimately deters the latter from doing so.

The aim of this chapter is to discuss the human rights concerns arising from the insertion of stabilization clauses in concession agreements. Section 4.2 discusses the compensation standards under international investment law. Section 4.3 will look at the human rights aspects concerning stabilization clauses. In so doing, this part of the chapter will examine three case studies: The MDA Agreement between Liberia and Mittal Steel Holdings AG, the Chad-Cameroon Pipeline Project, the Baku-Tbilisi-Ceyhan (BTC) Pipeline Project. Section 4.4 will consist of a conclusion.

4.2 Compensation standards under international investment law

The aim of this section is to discuss international compensation standards under international investment law. There is a general duty to pay compensation, once the host State has exercised its right to nationalize assets belonging to foreign investors.[8] This was illustrated in the *Upton Case*[9] where the arbitral tribunal upheld the right to nationalize.[10] However, in the tribunal also held that this right is inextricably linked to a duty to compensate the investor.[11] The aim of compensation is to eliminate all the consequences of the State's unilateral abrogation of the contract, which means restoring the investor to a position that they would have been in had the State not breached its agreement with the investor.[12]

Two standards of compensation prevail under international investment law: the "Hull Principle" and the "appropriate compensation" standard. The word

7 See Anita Schemberg, *Stabilization Clauses and Human Rights: A Research Project Conducted for IFC and United Nations Special Representative to the Secretary General on Business and Human Rights.* March 11 2008, 10.

8 Muna Ndulo, "The Nationalization of the Zambian Copper Industry" (1974) 6 *Zambia Law Journal* 55, 65; Paolo Vargiu, "Environmental Expropriation in International Investment Law" in Tullio Treves Francesco Seatzu and Seline Trevisanut (eds), *Foreign Investment and Common Concerns: An International Law Perspective* (Routledge 2013) 206–221, 206.

9 (1903) Ven Arb. 173.

10 Ibid 194.

11 Ibid.

12 Eduardo Jiménez de Aréchaga, "State Responsibility for the Nationalization of Foreign Owned Property" (1978) 11 *New York University Journal of International Law and Politics* 179, 180.

"adequate" under this standard suggests that the investor should not only be compensated for full market value of the nationalized property, but also for lost future profits (*lucrum cessans*).[13] Under the former standard, compensation payable must be "prompt, adequate and effective". Under the latter standard, compensation is determined on a case-by-case basis. This section discusses both standards and the issue of lost future profits.

4.2.1 The Hull principle

Under the Hull Principle, payment of compensation must be prompt, adequate and effective. The term "prompt" means that payment should be rendered within a "reasonable time".[14] As such, there should be no inordinate delays.[15] In addition to this, the interest rate payable to the investor must be not be one that negates the adequacy of the compensation. The term "effective" connotes that compensation payable to the investor must be made in a freely convertible currency and there should be no restriction on repatriation.[16] Finally, the term "adequate" suggests that the nationalizing State must restore the investor to a position they would have been in, had the nationalization not taken place. Not only does this mean paying the market value of the nationalized entity, there must also be a payment of lost future profits.[17]

The State Department of the United States, further elaborated on the meaning of the term "adequate" under the Hull Principle.[18] According to them, when property belonging to American investors is expropriated, then the host State must pay full market value of the said investors' assets. In their opinion, fair market value means calculating the compensation award to wipe out the consequences of the expropriation. In other words, that means calculating the compensation award, as if the expropriation has not occurred. This may sometimes be difficult to determine, in events that there have been no recent sales of comparable property. For this reason, the State Department uses three indirect valuation methods, in determining market value. These are: the going concern approach, the replacement cost approach and the book value approach.

The "going concern" approach bases the company's market value on its buying power.[19] Of course, there are instances where this approach may be deemed

13 See *AGIP v Congo* (1982) 21 ILM 726 and Richard J. Smith, "The United States Government Perspective on Expropriation and Investment in Developing Countries" (1976) 9 *Vanderbilt Journal of Transnational Law* 517, 519.

14 *Portugal v Germany* (1930) Ann Dig. Int'l L. Cases 150, 151.

15 Pamela B. Gann, "Compensation Standard for Expropriation" (1984) 23 *Columbia Journal of Transnational Law* 615, 620.

16 Restatement of the Foreign Relations Law of the United States (REVISED), §712, comment (Tent. Draft No. 3, 1982).

17 Smith (n 13) 519.

18 Smith (n 13) 519–520.

19 See also James Crawford, *The International Law Commission's Articles on State Responsibility, Introduction, Text and Commentaries* (Cambridge University Press 2002) 226.

impractical or unfair. This approach cannot, for example, reasonably be applied in instances where the investment has not been operational long enough to have an adequate profit history. The other difficulty with this method is that it is also susceptible to government manipulations that may actually distort the profitability of operations. Such manipulations include "increased taxes, threat of cancellation of contractual or concessionary rights, or withdrawals of privileges".[20]

Arbitral tribunals have certainly been cautious about awarding lost future profits, because they can be speculative. Thus, in the case of *CME v Czech Republic*,[21] Professor Brownlie asserted that compensation must reflect "the genuine value of the investments affected".[22] In his view, the genuine value of the investment must be compatible with a reasonable rate of return.[23] For this reason, Professor Brownlie awarded a sum of $160.9 million, in his separate opinion, which was, by his own admission, significantly lower than that rendered in the Final Award.[24] It is evident from this decision that even an arbitral tribunal can at times disagree on how to quantify loss to an investor.

The "replacement cost" approach is the second method utilized by the State Department in determining market value. Under this approach, the party determining the amount of compensation payable must look at the cost of replacing the property at the time of the expropriation "less actual depreciation".[25] The amount is not only greater than "book value", it also takes into account the earning power of the company, as manifested through projected future profits. This approach has been considered by the State Department as "generally less acceptable in most circumstances than the going-concern approach".[26] Furthermore, the State Department asserts that this method is rarely applicable in most instances of expropriation. It is only deemed useful in instances where identical replacements on the market to what has been taken exist. This rarely occurs, because assets that have been taken by the State are typically so unique, thus making it impossible to estimate the value of replacement.[27]

The "book value" approach entails valuing assets at the "acquisition cost less depreciation".[28] Because it bears little relationship to the actual value of the asset taken, it is the State Department's least preferred method of valuation.[29]

20 Smith (n 13) 520.

21 *CME v Czech Republic*, 31, Paragraph 69, http://italaw.com/sites/default/files/case-documents/ita0180.pdf.

22 Ibid 43, paragraph 106.

23 Ibid 45, paragraph 115.

24 Ibid 47, paragraph 121. The tribunal itself rendered an award of US $270 million.

25 Smith (n 13) 520.

26 Ibid.

27 Campbell McLachlan, Laurence Shore and Matthew Weiniger, *International Investment Arbitration: Substantive Principles* (OUP 2010) 319.

28 Smith (n 13) 520.

29 Ibid.

The applicability of the book value approach was illustrated in the case of *Asian Agricultural Ltd v Republic of Sri Lanka*.[30] The State in this case had a duty to provide full protection and security to the investment in question. However, they failed to do so. Consequently, armed insurgents destroyed a shrimp farm in which the investor had a 48% shareholding interest. The Tribunal in this case refused to order that the State pay for lost future profits. In the Tribunal's opinion:

> A reasonable prospective purchaser would, under these circumstances, be at least doubtful about the ability of the Company's balance sheet to cease being in the red, in the sense that the future earnings become effectively sufficient to off-set the past losses as well as to service the loans which exceed in their magnitude the Company's capital assets.[31]

The tribunal essentially opined that any potential buyer would have been rather sceptical about the company's ability to pull itself out of the red and whether future earnings could sufficiently offset past losses. Furthermore, loans the company had taken out were of greater value than the company's assets. Since the investor could not be compensated for any lost future profits, the tribunal drew up what they called a "comprehensive balance sheet".[32] This was done in order to reflect the investors' assets and liabilities, as derived from a list of the company's tangible assets.[33]

The book value approach is particularly problematic, because it disregards myriad factors which contribute to the value of a corporation, such as the "enterprises' contractual rights, know-how, goodwill, and management skills".[34] In addition to this, it only measures what is on the company's balance sheet, which is determined by applying standard accounting principles.[35] As such, it is the least preferred method in determining market value.[36]

The assessor must take all the circumstances of the case into account, when determining the valuation method applicable. This is in order to give the assessor enough leeway to apply one or a combination of methods, before finally arriving at a figure that will justly compensate the investor. The State Department also recognized that compensation could come in non-monetary forms, such as kickbacks and other services.[37]

30 *Asian Agricultural Ltd v Republic of Sri Lanka (Award) (1990) 4 ICSID Rep 245.*

31 Ibid 292.

32 Ibid 290.

33 Ibid 291.

34 McLachlan, Shore and Weiniger (n 27) 319.

35 Ibid 321. See also Paul D. Friedland and Eleanor Wong, "Measuring Damages for the Deprivation of Income-Producing Assets: ICSID Case Studies" (1991) 6 *ICSID Review Foreign Investment Law Journal* 400, 404.

36 Smith (n 13) 520.

37 Ibid.

4.2.2 Appropriate compensation

The other prevailing standard of compensation is the "appropriate compensation" method. Unlike the Hull Principle, there is no set formula for the determination of compensation.[38] Instead, compensation payable is determined on a case-by-case basis.[39] The advantage of this is that it accommodates all prevailing circumstances, when determining how much to compensate the investor.[40] This is a standard that has been endorsed by the United Nations General Assembly, the European Court of Human Rights, the House of Lords and the United States Court of Appeal (Second Circuit).[41]

The appropriate compensation standard is endorsed by the United Nations General Assembly in Resolution 1803 (1962). It is also endorsed in the Charter on the Economic Rights and Duties of States (CERDS).[42] General Assembly Resolution 1803 states that:

> 4. Nationalization, expropriation or requisitioning shall be based on grounds or reasons of public utility, security or the national interest which are recognized as overriding purely individual or private interests, both domestic and foreign. In such cases, the owner shall be paid appropriate compensation in accordance with the rules in force in the State taking such measures in the exercise of its sovereignty and in accordance with international law.[43]

United Nations General Assembly Resolution 1803 is notable, because it was endorsed by both developed and developing nations. In this instance, however, the United States took the term "appropriate" to mean "prompt, adequate, and effective". As such, in the United States' view, "appropriate" effectively was equivalent to the Hull Formula.[44]

Under the Charter on the Economic Rights and Duties of States, the right to nationalize is recognized, provided that appropriate compensation is paid, "taking into account its relevant laws and regulations and all circumstances that the State considers pertinent". Furthermore, the Charter on the Economic Rights and Duties of States provides that in the event where the issue of compensation

38 Rudolf Dolzer, "Expropriation for Nationalization" (1985) 8 *Encyclopedia of Public International Law* 214, 219 and Andra Eisenberg, "Different Constitutional Formulations of Compensation Clauses" (1993) 9 *South African Journal of Human Rights* 412, 418.

39 *Ebrahimi v Iran* (1994) 30 Iran-US CTR paragraphs 88 and 95, See also Jiménez de Aréchaga (n 12) 185.

40 Muthucumaraswamy Sornarajah, "Compensation for Expropriation. The Emergence of New Standards" (1979) 13 *Journal of World Trade Law* 108, 127–128.

41 See Eisenberg (n 38) 416–420.

42 General Assembly Resolution 3281 (XXIX) of 1974.

43 See also General Assembly Resolution 2158 (XXI) of 1966.

44 Stephen M. Schwebel, "The Story of the U.N.'s Declaration on Permanent Sovereignty over Natural Resources" (1963) 49 *American Bar Association Journal* 463, 465 and Junji Nakagawa, *Nationalization, Natural Resources and International Investment Law* (Routledge 2018) 136–137.

leads to controversy, the matter should as a general rule be settled under the national laws and tribunals of the host State.

Appropriate compensation was also endorsed by the European Court of Human Rights in *Lithgow v United Kingdom*.[45] In this case, one of the questions arising was whether the taking of property without payment of full compensation constituted a violation of Article I of the First Protocol of the European Convention on Human Rights. The European Court of Human Rights contended that:

> A decision to enact legislation will commonly involve consideration of various issues in which opinions within a democratic society may reasonably differ widely. Because of their direct knowledge of their society and its needs and resources, the national authorities are in principle better placed than the international judge to appreciate what measures are appropriate in this area and consequently the margin of appreciation available to them should be a wide one. It would, in the Court's view, be artificial in this respect to divorce the decision as to compensation terms from the actual decision to nationalise, since the factors influencing the latter will of necessity influence the former. Accordingly, the Court's power of review in the present case is limited to ascertaining whether the decisions regarding compensation fell outside the United Kingdom's wide margin of appreciation; it will respect the legislature's judgment in this connection unless that judgment was manifestly without reasonable foundation.[46]

Thus, the European Court of Human Rights effectively held that the right to nationalize by its very nature linked to the right to determine the amount of compensation payable. This is owing to the fact that the State is better placed to understand the needs of its society. Thus, the European Court of Human Rights declined to question the decision of the legislature, in the absence of reasonable grounds to do so.

Compensation standards were also considered by the House of Lords in the case of *Williams & Humbert v. W & T Trademarks*.[47] The case concerned the Spanish government, who had nationalized property belonging to an English family. The House of Lords endorsed the appropriate compensation standard and stated that it was applicable in the event of a nationalization. Lord Templeman opined that it was a firmly established principle that the State has the right to nationalize property and compensation had to be determined in this light.[48]

The United States Court of Appeals (Second Circuit) also endorsed the appropriate compensation standard, in the case of *Banco Nacional de Cuba v Chase Manhattan Bank*.[49] This was a case arising out of the Cuban nationalizations.

45 (1986) 8 EHRR 329.
46 Ibid 373.
47 [1986] AC 368.
48 Ibid 430–441.
49 658 F.2d 875 (2d Cir. 1981).

In this case, the Court held that failure to pay compensation was a violation of the law. The standard of compensation applicable, in their view, was that of "appropriate compensation". However, the court did assert "appropriate" could also mean "full". As such, the court opined that:

> It may well be the consensus of nations that full compensation need not be paid "in all circumstances" and that requiring an expropriating State to pay "appropriate compensation" – even considering the lack of precise definition of that term – would come closest to reflecting what international law requires. But, the adoption of an "appropriate compensation" requirement would not exclude the possibility that in some cases full compensation would be appropriate.[50]

This is very similar to the position taken under the World Bank Guidelines on the Treatment of Foreign Direct Investment. These guidelines endorse the appropriate compensation standard. However, they go on to say that compensation can only be deemed appropriate, if it is, "adequate, effective, and prompt".[51]

4.2.3 Lost future profits

From the preceding subsection, it has been seen that whether one adopts the Hull Principle or the appropriate compensation standard, lost future profits are invariably a factor considered when awarding compensation to the investor. The aim of this subsection is to discuss the case law concerning lost future profits. These are certainly a factor considered in determining the fair market value of property taken.[52] Although it has been advanced that lost future profits should only be considered when the taking is illegal,[53] case law seems to suggest otherwise. Arbitral tribunals have included lost future profits in the compensation package, even where the taking is deemed to be legal.[54] As such, arbitral tribunals make no distinction between legal and illegal takings. This is owing to the

50 Ibid 892–893. See also the World Bank Guidelines on the Treatment of Foreign Direct Investment. These guidelines endorse the appropriate compensation standard. However, they go on to say that compensation is only applicable if it is "adequate, effective and Prompt". See also Guideline IV, 1 and Guideline IV, 2 "World Bank Guidelines, on the Treatment of Foreign Direct Investment" (1992) 31 ILM 1379, 1382.

51 See also Guideline IV, 1 and Guideline IV, 2 "World Bank Guidelines, on the Treatment of Foreign Direct Investment" (1992) 31 ILM 1379, 1382.

52 *Phillips Petroleum Co. Iran v Islamic Republic of Iran* (1987) 21 Iran-US CTR 79, 123.

53 Derek W. Bowett, "State Contracts with Aliens: Contemporary Developments on Compensation for Termination or Breach" (1988) 49 *British Yearbook of International Law* 49, 63. See also Ian Brownlie, *Principles of Public International Law* (7th edn, OUP 2008) 539 and Irmgard Marboe, "Compensation and Damages in International Law: The Limits of "Fair Market Value' (2006) 7 *Journal of World Investment and Trade* 723.

54 See also Crawford (n 19) 226 and William C. Lieblich, "Determinations by International Tribunals of the Economic Value of Expropriated Enterprises" (1990) 7 *Journal of International Arbitration* 37, 47–48.

fact that the purpose of awarding compensation is to restore the investor to a position in which they would have been in, had the expropriation not taken place.[55] This was certainly the position taken in *Sapphire International Petroleum Ltd. v. National Iranian Oil Co. (NIOC)*[56] where the arbitral tribunal opined that:

> This rule is simply a direct deduction from the principle *pacta sunt servanda*, since its only effect is substitute a pecuniary obligation for the obligation which was promised but not performed. It is therefore natural that the creditor should thereby be given full compensation. This compensation includes loss suffered (*damnum emergens*), for example expenses incurred in performing the contract, and the profit lost (*lucrum cessans*), for example the net profit which the contract would have produced. The award of compensation for lost profit or the loss of a possible benefit has been frequently allowed by international tribunals.[57]

It can thus be seen that the aim of compensation is to wipe out the consequences of the expropriation and this not only includes compensating for loss suffered, it also includes payment of lost future profits. One of the early cases dealing with the issue of lost future profits was the *Case Concerning German interests in Upper Silesia.*[58] In this case, lost future profits were paid out because Poland had breached a Treaty, by taking over a company in which German nationals had rights. Such an action contravened Article 6 of the Geneva Convention Concerning Upper Silesia, which provided that:

> Poland may expropriate in Polish Upper Silesia in conformity with the provisions of Articles 7 to 23 undertakings belonging to the category of major industries including mineral deposits and rural estates. Except as provided in these clauses, the property, rights and interests of German nationals or of companies controlled by German nationals may not be liquidated in Polish Upper Silesia.

As such, although the Polish government ordinarily had the right to nationalize under this treaty, they could not exercise this right on property belonging to German nationals.[59] Article 7 of the Geneva Convention Concerning Upper Silesia further provided that during the fifteen years of acquiring sovereignty

55 *Sapphire International Petroleum Ltd v National Iranian Oil Co. (NIOC)* (1967) 36 ILR 136, 185–186.

56 Ibid.

57 Ibid 185–186.

58 For a comprehensive discussion of this case see Ronald E.M. Goodman and Yuri Parkhomenko, “Does the Chorzów Factory Standard Apply in Investment Arbitration? A Contextual Reappraial” (2017) 32 *ICSID Review* 304.

59 See *Case Concerning German Interests in Upper Silesia* (Chorzow Factory case), PCIJ Series A. No. 17, at 21.

over Polish Upper Silesia, the Polish government could only expropriate assets after the Upper Silesian Mixed Commission made a determination that the measure was indispensable to ensure the exploitation of such undertakings.[60]

Consequently, the German government initiated action against the Polish government in the Permanent Court of International Justice (PCIJ). The PCIJ held that the government has a general obligation to make reparations, in the event that it breaches an undertaking.[61] Such reparations in the courts view, "must, as far as possible, wipe out all the consequences of the illegal act and re-establish the situation which would have existed if that act had not been committed".[62] In their view, this included payment of lost future profits.[63]

Similarly, in the case of *Lena Goldfields v USSR*,[64] the International Court of Arbitration held that as a consequence of the latter repudiating their agreement with the former, the Soviet government had unjustly enriched themselves. Thus, in assessing damages the International Court of Arbitration awarded Lena Goldfields with a sum of GB£13 million. This figure implicitly included lost future profits, because Lena Goldfields had only made an initial investment of $20 million.[65]

Later tribunals determine lost future profits, by applying what is called the discounted cash flow (DCF) method. This entails examining current earnings and multiplying that figure by the remaining number of years still left on the cancelled contract and arrive at a figure. From this figure, the tribunal is to deduct any future payments that the nationalized entity had to make for the remainder of the contract. These include taxes, royalties and operating costs. In sum, projected expenditure is subtracted from projected gross earnings. An illustrating case of this is *LIAMCO v Libya*.[66] The tribunal certainly recognized Libya's international right to prematurely terminate a concession agreement. However, despite the taking being deemed legal, it did, however, constitute "source of liability to compensate the concessionaire".[67] This included the payment of lost future profits.[68] As such, the arbitrator thus opined that:

> In such confused state of international law, ... it appears clearly that there is no conclusive evidence of the existence of community or uniformity in principles between the domestic law of Libya and international law concerning

60 Goodman and Parkhomenko (n 58) 311.

61 *Case Concerning German Interests in Upper Silesia* (n 59) Ibid 29.

62 Ibid.

63 Ibid 52, see also *Starret Housing Corp v Islamic Republic of Iran* (1987) 16 Iran-US CTR 112, 196–201.

64 Arthur Nussbaum, "The Arbitration between the Lena Goldfields, Ltd. and the Soviet Government" (1950–51) 36 *Cornell Law Quarterly* 31, 42.

65 Jason W. Yackee, "Pacta Sunt Servanda and State Promises to Foreign Investors Before Bilateral Investment Treaties: Myth and Reality" (2009) 32 *Fordham International Law Journal* 1550, 1575.

66 (1981) 20 ILM 1, 81.

67 Ibid 60.

68 Ibid 81.

> the determination of compensation for nationalization in lieu of specific performance, and in particular concerning the problem whether or not all or part of the loss of profits (*lucrum cessans*) should be included in that compensation in addition to the damage incurred (*damnum emergens*).[69]

Thus, despite the fact that the nationalization was deemed legal, the arbitral tribunal still effectively recognized that loss of future profits ought to be made to LIAMCO. The value of the compensation was determined by an independent expert hired by LIAMCO. The first step the expert took was to estimate the amount of crude oil, liquids and gas that would have been produced for the remainder of the contract. This was then multiplied by the official prices which were subsisting in July 1976. This amount was not adjusted to take into account any future increases in market prices. They then deducted operating costs and any taxes and royalties from this amount. Such deductions were based on operating costs that existed prior to the nationalization measures taken in 1973. Furthermore, they applied a 12% discount factor to the net figure. Their evaluation came to $186,270,000.[70] This figure was reduced to $66,000,000.00 by the arbitrator as "equitable compensation". This was owing to the fact that it did not take into account currency inflation that was almost certain to occur.[71]

Lost future profits were also awarded by the arbitral tribunal in *Aminoil v Kuwait*[72] despite the nationalization being deemed legal. However, in so making their award, the arbitral tribunal examined all the circumstances of the case. They opined that the award had to be congruous with the legitimate expectations of the parties concerned.[73] In their view, "with reference to every long-term contract … there must necessarily be economic calculations, and the weighing-up of rights and obligations, of chances and risks, constituting the contractual equilibrium".[74] The Tribunal opined that AMINOIL's expectations were reflected in the 1973 agreement between the parties rather than the one formalized in 1948. This agreement had subsequently been modified by the Abu Dhabi Formula, which led to an increase in taxes and royalties payable to Kuwait.[75] It was further noted that AMINOIL had actually agreed to this formula. Therefore, the calculation of lost future profits had to take cognizance of this fact. For this reason, the amount awarded to AMINOIL was based on a reasonable rate of return and not the excessive one presented. As such, the award was based on the taxes and royalties reflected after 1973, rather than the ones reflected in the earlier agreement.[76]

69 Ibid 76.
70 Gann (n 15) 631.
71 (n 66) 160.
72 (1982) 21 ILM 976.
73 Ibid 1034, paragraph 148.
74 Ibid.
75 Ibid 1035, paragraph 154.
76 Ibid 1037–1038, paragraphs 160–163.

Lost future profits are also recognized in awards rendered by the International Centre for Settlement of Investment Disputes (ICSID) as evinced by the case of *AGIP v. Popular Republic of Congo.*[77] In this case, the government of Congo nationalized the claimant's interest in a Congolese company. The arbitral tribunal applied the law of Congo. The law of Congo incorporated elements of the French Code, which provided that lost future profits were recoverable.[78] The arbitral tribunal thus awarded lost future profits to AGIP.[79]

From the preceding case, it can thus be seen that the ICSID Tribunal also recognizes that lost future payments are included in compensation awards. However, arbitral tribunals are reluctant to award lost future profits in instances where lost future profits are impossible to determine. This typically occurs when the nationalized entity does not have a sufficient profit-making history. In such situations, any figure arrived at would be purely speculative, because there are no pre-existing figures to base it upon. For this reason, arbitral tribunals are typically reluctant to award lost future profits, in instances where an investor has no profit-making history. An illustrating case is that of *Benevuti et Bonfant v People's Republic of Congo.*[80]

In this case, the Congolese government had nationalized a company in which Benevuti et Bonfant (B&B), an Italian company, had a 40% equity interest.[81] Under an agreement with the Congolese government, B & B were to build a bottle manufacturing plant in Congo.[82] Although plant production commenced in 1975, the owners of the corporation left Congo the following year. This was upon advice from the Italian Embassy that their safety was in jeopardy.[83] Subsequently, the Congolese army proceeded to occupy the plant. Although there was no formal act of expropriation, B & B argued that the actions of the Congolese government effectively took over their interest in the operation.

The arbitral tribunal decided the dispute *ex aequo et bono* (in justice and fairness), pursuant to Article 42(3) of the ICSID Convention.[84] B & B contended in their submissions that the value of its 40% ownership interest was CFA 110,098,936. This figure was arrived at by taking into account lost future profits, which they expected to make over the period for which the agreement was supposed to subsist.[85]

The arbitral tribunal appointed an independent expert to make the valuation. The independent expert took the view that future profits could not be included

77 (1982) 21 ILM 726.
78 Ibid 737, paragraphs 98–100.
79 Ibid 739 paragraph 115, section (a)(ii)(D).
80 (1982) 21 ILM 740.
81 Ibid 748, paragraph 2.6.
82 Ibid 749, paragraph 2.9.
83 Ibid 751, paragraph 2.23.
84 Ibid 752, paragraph 4.4 and 758 paragraph 4.65.
85 Ibid 759, paragraph 4.75.

in the award because no profits had actually been realized by the company during its one year of operation. Since their profit-making history was virtually non-existent, the expropriated company was treated as a start-up, rather than a fully operational entity. The expert, then, made an evaluation on the basis of the most objective criteria at the time. This was the actual amount of the original investment, multiplied by B & V's 40% interest. From this, the expert came to a valuation of CFA 122,000,000. This actually exceeded the amount claimed by B & B.[86]

Although the tribunal agreed, in principle, with the expert's opinion, they lowered the amount to CFA 110,098,936, which was the original amount claimed. This was owing to the fact that the valuation of the expert exceeded the amount originally claimed by B & B.[87] The arbitral tribunal also added interest. This was to be calculated from the day that the taking took place. Although B & B had originally requested an interest rate of 15%, the tribunal lowered this to 10%, which as the interest rate that that Congolese government had used in their counterclaims. In so doing, the arbitral tribunal was exercising its authority to decide the matter *ex aequo et bono*. As such they accordingly opined that, under the circumstances, a rate of 10% was equitable.[88]

The position taken in *Benevuti et Bonfant v People's Republic of Congo* can be contrasted with the latter case of *SOABI v Senegal*,[89] where the arbitral tribunal included lost future profits in their compensation award, despite the fact that SOABI had not yet started making profits. This case is certainly consistent with earlier non-ICSID awards, such as *Delagoa Bay and East African Railway*[90] and *Sapphire International*.[91] In the *Delagoa* case, the Portuguese government had annulled a railroad concession, prior to the commencement of operations.[92] Despite this fact, the tribunal still awarded lost future profits. Similarly, in *Sapphire International* the tribunal held that the claimant was entitled to lost future profits, despite the fact that the area in dispute had not yet been prospected. However, tribunals since the SOABI award was rendered have invariably been reluctant to award lost future profits, in instances where there has been no profit making history.[93] As such, the SOABI case is more the exception than the norm.[94]

86 Ibid 760, paragraph 4.78.

87 Ibid 760, paragraph 4.79.

88 Ibid 762, paragraph 4.98.

89 *Société Ouest Africaine des Bétons Industriels v State of Senegal* (1988) 2 ICSID Rep 164.

90 *United States and Great Britain v Portugal* (1900) quoted in Majorie M. Whiteman, *Damages in International Law: Volume 3* (United States Government Printing Office 1943) 1694, 1697.

91 *Sapphire International* (n 55) 187–188.

92 Whiteman Ibid 1697.

93 See *Tecnicas Medioambientales Tecmed SA v United Mexican States* (2004) 43 ILM 133, 183, see also *Wena Hotels Ltd v Arab Republic of Egypt* (2000) 6 ICSID Rep 67, *Biloune and Marine Drive Complex Ltd v Ghana Investments Centre and the Government of Ghana* (1990) 95 ILR 183.

94 McLachlan, Shore and Weiniger (n 27) 325.

It is clear from the foregoing that no clear consensus exists on which standard of compensation is applicable in international investment law.[95] The Hull Principle is not universally accepted.[96] However, it is adopted in a plethora of Bilateral Investment Treaties.[97] Furthermore, even when arbitral tribunals do not explicitly endorse the Hull Principle, awards rendered seem to reflect the tenets of the Hull Principle. This is particularly so, when arbitral tribunals include lost future profits in their awards. As such, even in instances where the appropriate compensation standard is applied, the effect of those decisions reflects the tenets of the Hull Principle.[98]

Awarding of lost future profits is advantageous, in that it protects the investor's legitimate expectations. This is because it essentially means that investors are able to realize the profits they had projected to make from the entity, despite the State unilaterally abrogating its agreement with the investor. However, lost future profits make it more onerous for the State to pursue its legitimate public functions. This includes its right to advance new human rights laws and also its right to uphold its international human rights obligations.

4.3 Stabilization clauses and human rights obligations

It has been seen from the preceding section that breach of a concession agreement means that the host State must compensate the investor. If there is stabilization clause in the concession clauses then this elicits a legitimate expectation on the part of the investor. As such, when determining lost future profits, arbitral tribunals will invariably calculate them based on the number of years left on the contract. This is because the investor would have expected the contract to subsist for the period stipulated therein. The difficulty with this, however, arises when the host State wishes to pass new human rights legislation. The aim of this section is to critically examine the case law pertaining to stabilization and human rights.

95 Rudolph Dolzer, "New Foundations of the Law of Expropriation of Alien Property" (1981) 75 *American Journal of International Law* 553, 553.

96 See Oscar Schachter, "Compensation for Expropriation" (1984) 78 *American Journal of International Law* 121–130 and Frank G. Dawson and Burns H. Weston, "Prompt, Adequate and Effective: A Universal Standard of Compensation?" (1962) 32 *Fordham Law Review* 727.

97 Andreas F. Lowenfeld, *International Economic Law* (n 10) 564, McLachlan, Shore and Weiniger (n 31) 317 and Wenshua Shan, "Is Calvo Dead?" (2007) 55 *American Journal of Comparative Law* 123. See also Wenshua Shan and Norah Gallagher, "China" in Chester Brown (ed), *Commentaries on Selected Model Investment Treaties* (OUP, 2013) 164–165 which discusses the Chinese Model BIT. Even though it avoids language such as 'adequate' as per the Hull Formula, the actual calculation methods prescribed are not substantially different the aforementioned standard of compensation.

98 Gann (n 15) 618 and M.H. Mendelson, "Compensation for Expropriation: The Case Law" (1985) 79 *American Journal of International Law* 414, 415.

4.3.1 The MDA agreement between Liberia and Mittal Steel Holdings AG

The first case study concerns the Mineral Development Agreement between the Government of Liberia and Mittal Steel Holdings AG. The National Transitional Government of Liberia (NTGL) had concluded a Mineral Development Agreement with Mittal Steel Holdings AG, which was a Swiss Based transnational corporation on 17 August 2005. According to this agreement, Mittal Steel is to exploit Liberia's vast resources of iron ore. It was anticipated that there would be investments of US$900 million over a period of twenty-five years. This was a foreign investment contract, which would contribute to the development of Liberia's economy, lower unemployment, increase revenues and improve Liberia's transport network and infrastructure.

The difficulty with this agreement, however, was that the stabilization clause militated against certain human rights obligations, which should be fulfilled by the State and also by the corporation and its employees.[99] Article XIX, section 9, page 21 effectively provided that:

> (...) In particular, any modifications that could be made in the future to the Law as in effect on the Effective Date shall not apply to the CONCESSIONAIRE and its Associates without their prior written consent, but the CONCESSIONAIRE and its Associates may at any time elect to be governed by the legal and regulatory provisions resulting from changes made at any time in the Law as in effect on the Effective Date.
>
> In the event of any conflict between this Agreement or the rights, obligations and duties of a Party under this Agreement, and any other Law, including administrative rules and procedures and matters relating to procedure, and applicable international law, then this Agreement shall govern the rights, obligations and duties of the Parties.

Effectively, this clause represents a regulatory stabilization clause. In principle, such a clause should only have provided Mittal with a level of protection that would enable it to operate in a stable regulatory environment. However, the provisions in the Mineral Development Agreement between Mittal Steel Holdings AG and the Government of Liberia go much further than this. This is owing to the fact that although the agreement recognized that Mittal Steel is subject to domestic law, this is a narrower range of laws and actually applies elsewhere in Liberia.

It would seem that, under this provision, if Mittal Steele could show that government action has prejudiced the rights it has been granted, then the former could object to the application of existing Liberian laws as interpreted by Liberian courts and applied elsewhere in the county. In addition to this, Mittal

99 Jernej Letnar Cernic, "Corporate Human Rights Obligations under Stabilization Clauses" (2010) 11 *German Law Journal* 210, 217.

Steel could also refuse to consent to the application of any new laws that have been passed, as long as the concession subsists. The difficulty with this position is that a State like Libya would have seen investment as a matter of great importance. Given this fact, the agreement would effectively deter the Government of Liberia from exercising its legitimate public functions, including the right to regulate. On the other hand, a company like Mittal is in a position to choose which new laws it will comply with.

Furthermore, one of the issues highlighted is the fact that Liberia was trying to rebuild itself, after a long war. As such, it was anticipated that there would be some much-needed legal reforms in Liberia. For example, in 2003, the International Legal Assistance Consortium had conducted a review of Liberia's judicial system. It concluded that there was need for both short- and long-term legal reform.[100] In addition to this, Global Witness had interviewed the United Nations Mission in Liberia (UNMIL) who had indicated that they would be providing international assistance to facilitate the review and updating of Liberian legislation.[101] Furthermore, Global Witness had also interviewed a senior figure in the Ministry of Labour, who had indicated that existing Liberian labour laws dated from the 1970s.[102]

It was noted by Global Witness that the stabilization clauses may have far-reaching consequences.[103] This is owing to the fact that they could severely limit the Government of Liberia's ability to fulfil both current and future obligations under the Liberian Constitution, domestic law and international law. This also includes the implementation of international treaty obligations. For example, clauses in the Mineral Development Agreement with Mittal prevent the application of existing or new laws, that will "derogate from or otherwise prejudice" Mittal's rights under the agreement. This effectively means that the Liberia would be prevented from relying on its own Constitution, since it falls under the agreement's definition of "law". As Global Witness observed:

> Such restrictions on constitutional prerogatives would not be accepted by governments in the developed world. The provisions would not be enforceable in English law, for instance, under the principle that the Crown cannot contract to fetter its own discretion or that the State cannot remove its own freedom of choice when it comes to acting in the public's benefit or interest.[104]

The stabilization clause is further compounded by the fact that Article XXI, section 3, page 22 of the concession, also provides that the government is to indemnify the Concessionaire for all "claims, liabilities, costs, expenses, losses

100 International Legal Assistance Consortium, Liberia, December 2003.

101 Global Witness interview with senior UNMIL official, April 2006.

102 Global Witness interview with senior member of the Ministry of Labour, April 2006.

103 Ibid 31.

104 Ibid.

and damage" as a result of the Government of Liberia's failure to honour the concession agreement. Thus, any breach of the concession agreement would have pecuniary consequences. The fact that there would be financial consequences attached to Liberia's desire to implement new human rights legislation effectively causes the government of the aforementioned country to think twice about doing so.

4.3.2 The Chad-Cameroon Pipeline Project

The Chad-Cameroon Pipeline Project in 2005 also brought intense debate on stabilization clauses and their impact on human rights. This project was divided into two parts. The first part involved the extraction of oil and the drilling of approximately three hundred wells in Chad. The second part involved the export of the oil, through a pipeline which ran from the Doba fields in Chad to Kribi in Cameroon.[105] This project was certainly agreed to by both the governments of Cameroon and Chad. It was also agreed to by the host States of the corporations involved. Investors in this project included corporations such as ExxonMobil, US Chevron which were US corporations and Petronas which was a Malaysian State-owned oil company. In addition to this, financing for the project was supported by a number of private investors, banks and export credit agencies. The World Bank also considered the project "as a means of bringing about economic development and "poverty alleviation" in both Chad and Cameroon – and especially Chad".

The major concern here was the impact that the project would have on human rights in countries such as Cameroon, because of the long history of severe human rights abuses in both countries. This was further compounded by several reports of corruption and human rights abuses surrounding the project. As such, there were certainly concerns as to whether this investment would have an adverse impact on human rights in Chad and Cameroon for many years to come. Amnesty International observed that the contractual duties that had been imposed under the investment agreement would effectively prevent both the governments of Chad and Cameroon from fulfilling their international human rights obligations.[106]

Although there were several legal instruments governing the terms of the investment between Chad, Cameroon, and the Consortium of other parties, the most important for the purposes of this book are four investment agreements. The development of oilfields in Chad was governed by two agreements. The first was a 1988 agreement between the Consortium and Chad. It was meant to run for an initial period of thirty-five years, with the possibility of extension for a further thirty-five years. The second agreement a 2004 agreement between the

105 Amnesty International, *Contracting Out of Human Rights – The Chad Pipeline Project* (Amnesty International 2005) 13.

106 Ibid 7.

same parties. This also regulated the development of oilfields and had the same duration as the 1988 agreement, with the possibility of further extension.

The construction and development of the pipeline between Chad and Cameroon was also governed by two agreements. The first was the 1997 COTCO-Cameroon agreement, which was to run for a period of twenty-five years, with the possibility of extension for a further twenty-five years. The second was the 1998 TOTCO-Chad agreement, which was to run for thirty years and could be extended until the expiration of the last concession.

To ensure that these contracts subsisted for the period stipulated and could be undertaken with a degree of legal predictability, stabilization clauses were included in these agreements. The purpose of these was to ensure that domestic law would not be applicable to the project, without their express consent. In the event that national law conflicted with the provisions of the agreements, then the latter would take precedence. An example of the stabilization clauses was that in Article 21.3 of the TOTCO-Chad agreement, which provided that:

> During the term of this Convention, the Republic of Chad guarantees that no governmental act taken after December 19, 1988 will be applied to TOTCO, without prior agreement between the Parties, which has the duty established effect of increasing, directly, indirectly or by virtue of its application to the Shareholders, the obligations and charges imposed by this Convention or which has the effect of adversely affecting the rights and economic benefits of TOTCO or of Shareholders as provided for in this Convention, including the effect duly established and passed on to TOTCO of the adverse effect on the charges of Affiliates or of the Contractors as a result of such act.[107]

Furthermore, all disputes arising from the project were to be settled through international arbitration. Domestic law was also to be interpreted by the arbitrators, in a way that does not economically disadvantage the consortium.[108] Moreover, by virtue of the agreement, the projects were immune from both international law and the domestic law of the host States concerned. Instead, the provided that the project is to be carried out in conformity with "the relevant national petroleum code and ordinary laws that do not conflict with the project agreement" and "the operating standards generally acceptable in the international petroleum industry".[109]

The difficulty with these provisions is that they are incongruous with the Chad and Cameroon's obligations under international law. Both nations had ratified a plethora of both regional and international treaties, which imposed a number of human rights obligations. Furthermore, they had adhered to

107 Translated from French in Amnesty International (n 105) 22.
108 Ibid 23.
109 Ibid 24.

International Labour Organization (ILO) standards and were bound by human rights obligations under customary international law. In addition to this, both countries had incorporated the UN Charter, the Universal Declaration on Human Rights and the African Charter on Human and Peoples' Rights, under their constitutions. As such, both nations had human rights obligations, both under national and international law. This meant taking all appropriate measures to fulfil these rights, including taking measures preventing third parties such as foreign investors, from interfering with those rights.[110] Amnesty International also observed that the corporations under this project, "like all non-State actors in society ..." had a duty "to operate in a responsible manner, and this includes respecting human rights".[111]

It has been seen that Chad and Cameroon had a very weak system of human rights recognition. This, combined with the use of stabilization clauses adversely affects the State's position to fulfil its human rights obligations both at a national and international level. In effect, this means that the State has to rely on the corporation to respect human rights on a "more or less voluntary basis".[112] As such, it would appear that under these investment agreements, company codes of conduct and promises of high standards, which should only come as assurances over and above national law, now seem to supersede State regulation of investment projects.[113]

4.3.3 The BTC pipeline project

Another example of stabilization clauses effectively clashing with State's obligation to uphold both national and international human rights is the BTC Pipeline Project.[114] This project involves a 1,768 km pipeline system to carry "one million barrels of crude oil per day" from the Azeri-Chirag-Guneshli fields to Ceyhan on the Turkish Mediterranean coast.[115]

It was developed by a consortium of eleven oil companies consisting of BP (30.10%), SOCAR (25.00%), Chevron (8.90%), Statoil (8.71%), Tpao (6.53%), Eni (5.00%), Total (5.00%), Itochu (3.40%), Inpex (2.50%), ConcoPhillips (2.50%) and Amerada Hess (2.36).[116] This consortium was brought together in the Baku-Tbilisi-Ceyhan Pipeline Company (BTC Co).

110 Ibid 18.

111 Ibid 19.

112 Sandra Helgadottir Ingolfsson, *Stabilization Clauses in Investment Agreements – A Human Rights and Development Perspective* (Graduate Thesis Master of Laws Programme, Lund 2012) 50.

113 Amnesty International (n 105) 12.

114 See generally Terre-Eve Lawson Remer, "A Role of the IFC in Integrating Environmental & Human Rights Standards into Care Project Covenants: A Case Study of the Baku-Tbilisi-Ceyhan Oil Project" in *Global Working Paper 01/05 Symposium*. 'Transnational and Human Rights' NYU School of Law.

115 Ibid 9, 10–11.

116 http://www.btc.com.tr/proje.html.

This project was governed by the Intergovernmental Agreement (IGA) between Georgia, Azerbaijan and Turkey and the Host Government Agreements (HGA), which were signed in September 1999 and in October 2000 by the consortium of oil companies, as well as host governments of participating governments.[117] The stabilization clause in the Host Government Agreements is introduced in two parts. The first part refers to the State's obligation to restore the economic equilibrium, in the event that the project is affected by a "Change in Law". The stabilization clause thus provides that:

> 7.2 The Government hereby covenants and agrees (on its behalf and acting on behalf of and committing the State Authorities) that throughout the term of this agreement.
>
> vi. 'If any domestic or international agreement or treaty; any legislation, promulgation, enactment, decree, accession or allowance; any other form of commitment, policy or pronouncement or permission, has the effect of impairing, conflicting or interfering with the implementation of the Project, or limiting, abridging or adversely affecting the value of the Project or any of the rights, privileges, exemptions, waivers, indemnifications or protections granted or arising under this Agreement or any other Project Agreement it shall be deemed a Change in Law under Article 7.2(xi).

Second, the State has an obligation to compensate the investors in the event that newly introduced legal requirements adversely affect the value or economic equilibrium of the project. Therefore, if legislative changes interfere with the economic equilibrium of the Project, then the investor must be paid compensation. The clause thus states that:

> the Government shall provide monetary compensation as provided in Article 10 for any loss or damage which is caused or arises from: ... (iii) any failure by the State Authorities, whether as a result of action or inaction, to maintain Economic Equilibrium as provided in Section 7.2(xi).

The stabilization clause is certainly couched in very broad terms and has attracted intense criticism from organizations such as Amnesty International. The first observation made by Amnesty International is that the project could last as long as sixty years. Thus, the human rights implications of this project are far-reaching. It was noted it would make it harder for Turkey to sign up fully to international standards. Amnesty International argued that Turkey may have to find itself entering reservations and exempting the pipeline from any new international undertakings it makes.[118] Consequently, those affected by the project

117 Jernej Letnar Cernic, "Corporate Human Rights Obligations under Stabilization Clauses" (2010) 11 *German Law Journal* 210, 220.

118 Amnesty International, *Human Rights on the Line: The Baku-Tbilisi-Ceyhan Pipeline Project* (Amnesty International UK 2003) 16.

will be pushed more deeply into second class status. In the alternative, Turkey may push decide to push ahead and apply the new standards". However, this would mean that Turkey could face a heavy claim for damages from the consortium. Given this prospect, there is a potential that Turkey would be less inclined to meet its human rights obligations.

4.4 Conclusion

It could thus be concluded that stabilization clauses aim to insulate investors from non-commercial risks associated with foreign investment. In the event that a State unilaterally abrogates a contract with an investor, the latter's legitimate expectations are taken into account when determining the amount of compensation payable.

The duty to pay compensation in the event that a State breaches an investment agreement is unquestionable. It has been seen that there are two compensation standards under international investment law. These are the Hull Principle and the appropriate compensation standard. This chapter has discussed what standard entails. Further, it has been established that both standards of compensation recognize that lost future profits are typically considered, when rendering the compensation award.

This chapter has also established that stabilization clauses do raise human rights concerns. It has been seen stabilization clauses are certainly a source of liability for States who wish to develop and implement their human rights obligations. This is owing to the fact that compliance with new human rights obligations imposed by the State, may add to the operating costs of foreign investors. Consequently, the State would have to compensate the investor for these additional costs.

For countries like the Republic of Zambia, this may have far-reaching consequences for the development of human rights. Over the past decade, the Republic of Zambia has made great strides in the area of gender equity and equality by implementing various pieces of legislation. The aim of the next chapter is to discuss these, in the context of the stabilization clauses contained in development agreements between the government and copper mining companies operating in Zambia.

5 Stabilization clauses and gender equality

A case study of Zambia

5.1 Introduction

The Republic of Zambia is a country located in Southern Africa. It has a population of just over 15 million.[1] As one of the world's major copper producers, Zambia's economy is pegged primarily on copper.[2] In 2012, for example, the mining industry accounted for 86% of foreign direct investment into the Republic of Zambia, 80% of the country's export earnings and 25% of all revenues collected by government.[3] Thus because Zambia is a mono-economy, copper is treated as the national asset that will foster development and economic prosperity in Zambia. As such, mining in Zambia is of economic, social and political importance.[4]

Copper mining in Zambia has undergone three major transitions since mining operations commenced in the 1920s.[5] The mining industry in Zambia was under private hands, before being nationalized in the 1970s and falling under the hands of the State-owned Zambia Consolidated Copper Mines (ZCCM).[6] Simultaneously, Zambia became a one-party State. Subsequently to this, the mining industry declined due to low copper prices and outright mismanagement.[7] As such, the mines became a loss-making burden on the national treasury.[8] This

1 Phenny Mwaanga, Mathews Silondwa, George Kasali and Paul M. Banda, "Preliminary Review of Mine Air Pollution in Zambia" (2019) 5 Heliyon https://www.sciencedirect.com/science/article/pii/S2405844019361456.

2 Andrew Sardanis, *A Venture in Africa: The Challenges of African Business* (I.B. Tauris 2007) 244.

3 Jackson Sikamo, Alex Mwanza and Cade Mweemba, "Copper Mining in Zambia – History and Future" (2016) 116 *Journal of the Southern African Institute of Mining and Metallurgy* 491, 494.

4 Muna Ndulo, "Mining Legislation and Mineral Development in Zambia" (1986) 19 *Cornell International Law Journal* 1, 5.

5 Antony Martin, *Mining their Own Business: Zambia's Struggle against Western Control* (Hutchinson 1972) 30.

6 Savior Mwambwa, Aaron Griffiths and Andreas Kahler, *A Fool's Paradise? Zambia's Mining Tax Regime* (Centre for Trade Policy and Development 2010) 5.

7 Sangwani Patrick Ng'ambi, "Mineral Taxation and Resource Nationalism in Zambia" (2015) 2 *Southern African Journal of Policy and Development* 6, 6.

8 Christian von Soest "How Does Neopatrimonialism Affect the African State's Revenues? The Case of Tax Collection in Zambia" (2007) 45 *Journal of Modern African Studies* 621, 636.

led to calls by the International Monetary Fund and the World Bank, to privatize the mines owned by ZCCM.[9]

When Zambia returned to multiparty democracy in the 1990s, the mines were privatized. The government also sought to attract foreign direct investment into the mining industry so as to resuscitate it. To foster this, the government passed various pieces of legislation including the Mines and Minerals Act 1995, which enabled them to enter into "Development Agreements" with foreign investors. These agreements contained various tax incentives within them. To protect those incentives and to ensure that the Development Agreements subsisted for the stipulated timeframe, various stabilization clauses were inserted therein.

The previous chapter, discussed the impact of stabilization clauses on the development of human rights. Under this case study, we take previous legal scholarship on the subject a bit further, by discussing the impact of stabilization clauses on the development of gender laws in the Republic of Zambia. This is particularly against the backdrop of new pieces of legislation, such as the Gender Equity and Equality Act, No. 22 of 2015 and the Employment Code Act, No. 3 of 2019. These are important as they create new gender obligations on the investor. These will be of primary concern to the investor because any new legal developments in gender policy either loosen or tighten existing obligations. In either scenario, there will be monetary implications. If these obligations have a material adverse effect on the profits of mining companies, then this may create an obligation on the government to compensate them.

This chapter uses Zambia as a case study to explore the obligations which are required of investors as result of legal development in the State's gender policy. Section 5.2 examines the relevance of gender outcomes for investment. Section 5.3 will look at the legal framework for gender equality in Zambia. Thereafter, this chapter will be looking at the themes and obligations in the gender and investment framework. Section 5.5 will then look at the implications of the stabilization clauses in the Development Agreements, before arriving at a conclusion.

5.2 Relevance of gender outcomes for investment

In 2015, the United Nations adopted the 2030 Agenda for Sustainable Development (**"Agenda 2030"**).[10] By this agenda, the nations of the world committed to a plan of action for people, planet and prosperity.[11] States agree to 17 Sustainable Development Goals (**"SDGs"**); each of which has unique targets

9 John Lungu, "Copper Mining Agreements in Zambia: Renegotiation or Law Reform?" (2008) 117 *Review of African Political Economy* 403, 405.

10 See "Transforming Our World: The 2030 Agenda for Sustainable Development" Resolution adopted by the General Assembly on 25 September 2015 A/RES/70/1, available at https://www.un.org/ga/search/view_doc.asp?symbol=A/RES/70/1&Lang=E.

11 Ibid.

which must be achieved. The fifth of the SDGs is to achieve gender equality and empower all women and girls.[12]

SDG number five includes in its targets ending all forms of discrimination against all women and girls everywhere.[13] States are also required to adopt and strengthen sound policies and enforceable legislation for the promotion of gender equality and the empowerment of all women and girls at all levels. It is against this background that the rationale for investors should take note of changes in gender policy. There are at least three reasons why gender policy is relevant for modern international investment law: (1) It clarifies targets for sustainability of investments, (2) it present opportunities for co-operation between the public and private sector, and (3) it fosters predictability in policy over the period of the investment. These points are each discussed, in turn.

5.2.1 Gender policy clarifies targets for sustainability of investments

In the twenty-first century, virtually all investments expected to meet the three-fold arms of sustainability. Investments are required to be commercially, economically and environmentally sustainable. At times, the competition between these needs can make it unclear exactly how an investment can be made more sustainable.

The development of the SDGs assists States and investors gain some clarity as to the modern understanding of sustainability as a pursuit in business. Gender equality is listed among the SDGs[14] and the targets set out there can serve as a guide for policy development.

With gender being so such a priority at international level, investors whether foreign or local would do well to note the gender obligations imposed by domestic laws. In the case of in Zambia, there is the Gender Equity and Equality Act,[15] which shows what is expected of the private sector. There are also gender-related obligations under the Employment Code[16] serve only as minimum standards which investors can use to develop their own codes.

Ideally, the investors' compliance with domestic legislation and the State's enforcement of stated gender objectives should contribute to a more sustainable investment climate. In a country like Zambia, however, the institutional capacity for enforcement is still limited. Thus, the private sector investors are expected to lead the way in developing the sustainability of their investments. Such an arrangement can only work in the context of greater investor-State co-operation.

12 Ibid.

13 See SDG 5.1.

14 SDG number 5.

15 Gender Equity and Equality Act No. 22 of 2015.

16 Act No. 10 of 2019.

5.2.2 Opportunities for investor-State co-operation

There are at least two ways that the gender obligations set out in a legal framework present opportunities for co-operation between the public and private sector. First, due to the global drive for women empowerment, investors have the opportunity to tap into a human resource representing a larger portion of the society. Second, the private sector's expertise can help bridge the gap in the State's enforcement capacity; enabling the private sector to set the pace at which gender goals are achieved.

The self-interest of investors may present the danger in allowing the private sector to shape enforcement of policy in this manner.[17] However, a balance can be achieved by the involvement of civil society organizations which already assist in monitoring corporate behaviour.[18] In this manner, if investors prioritize the obligations drawn from the legal framework, they can lead in the achievement of gender objectives. This contributes to the overall sustainability of the investment climate. The investment climate is also improved where policy changes are more predictable to investors; a factor that may make gender-related obligations more acceptable.

5.2.3 Predictability of policy over the period of investment

The stability of investment policy is a key driver of investment, especially for a developing country like Zambia.[19] Investors are increasingly sensitive about the impact which obligations introduced by new laws may have on the bottom line. Due to their onerous nature, the gender obligations in the Zambian legal framework will require financial commitment from investors seeking to be compliant and proactive in the pursuit of gender related objectives.

The benefit of monitoring the changes in gender policy, however, is that investors can use the policy goals of the State to predict what further measures could be put in place. For instance, reading legislation and policy could serve as a reference point for any affirmative action measure which the State may put in place.

The above are not intended to be a comprehensive list of reasons why investors must take note of changes in gender policy. However, they do serve as motivation for taking note of the changes in the legal framework ahead of the discussion of the Zambia's framework for gender and investments.

17 For criticism for the self-interested business management strategies even for companies seeking to do good in society, see Andrew Crane, Guido Palazzo and Laura J. Spence, "Contesting the Value of 'Creating Shared Value'" (2014) 56 *California Management Review* 130, 149.

18 See Michael Porter and Mark Kramer, "Creating Shared Value: How to Reinvent Capitalism and Unleash a Wave of Innovation and Growth" (2011) 89 *Harvard Business Review* 1, 13.

19 For a discussion on stability and the right to regulate see Lorenzo Cotula, "Reconciling Regulatory Stability and Evolution of Environmental Standards in Investment Contracts: Towards a Rethink of Stabilization Clauses" (2008) 1 *Journal of World Energy and Business* 158.

5.3 Legal framework for gender and investment

Zambia is one of the signatories of the UN's Agenda 2030 and a number of other international instruments which promote gender equality at global and regional level. Zambia thus serves as a good case study to understand the interplay between gender policy and international law. An overview of the legal framework is presented by way of summary of key domestic and international sources. The criteria for selecting sources was the direct contribution these sources make to the interplay between gender policy and investment law.

5.3.1 Domestic sources of law and policy

5.3.1.1 The constitution and statutes

As a result of its Supremacy Clause,[20] the Constitution of Zambia ranks highest in the hierarchy of domestic sources of investment law. As such, all statutes and case law are only valid to the extent of their compliance with the constitution. The Constitution also embodies the Bill of Rights from which all investors draw protection for their investments.

The first of the statutes relevant to investment is the Lands Acquisition Act.[21] The stated purpose of this Act according to its Preamble is "*to make provision for the compulsory acquisition of land and other property*". This Preamble extends the scope of the Act beyond immovable property (as its name suggests) and makes the Act applicable to the expropriation of moveable property such as shares. The whole Act is dedicated to determining how and when expropriation can take place. Key provisions as regards expropriation include the empowering and procedural provisions which are housed in Part II (sections 3–9). The provisions of this Act are supplemented by the provisions of the Zambia Development Agency Act.[22]

Developed under the direction of Zambia's Ministry of Gender,[23] the Gender Equity and Equality Act[24] ("**GEEA**") domesticates international human rights documents, such as the United Nation's Convention on the Elimination of all forms of Discrimination Against Women ("**CEDAW**"),[25] the Protocol to the African Charter on Human and People's Rights on the Rights of Women in Africa Towards Gender Equality ("**Maputo Protocol**")[26] and the Southern African Development Community Protocol on Gender and Development, 2008

20 See Article 2.

21 Chapter 189 of the Law of Zambia.

22 Act No. 11 of 2006.

23 Country Gender Profile: Zambia Final Report March 2016 Japan International Cooperation Agency (JICA) Japan Development Service Co., Ltd. (JDS).

24 Gender Equity and Equality Act [No. 22 of 2015].

25 General Assembly resolution 34/180 of 18 December 1979.

26 Adopted by the 2nd Ordinary Session of the Assembly of the Union, Maputo, 11 July 2003, available at https://www.un.org/en/africa/osaa/pdf/au/protocol_rights_women_africa_2003.pdf.

(**"SADC Protocol"**).[27] This Act has yet to come into force as the Minister responsible for Gender has not passed the necessary law to give it legal effect.[28] However, the provisions of this Act are still worth noting for the sake of understanding the landscape for gender and investment in Zambia.

The Employment Code[29] is the most recent legislation reflecting measures which investors should be aware of as regards gender. This Act is Zambia's principal labour legislation and has introduced drastic changes to labour law as a whole and gender policy in particular. The understanding of these statutes can be supplemented by reference to the policies developed by the executive arm of Zambia's government.

5.3.1.2 The 7th National Development Plan

The 7th National Development Plan (**"7th NDP"**) and the National Gender Policy (**"NGP"**) do not constitute sources of law in the classical sense. However, as overarching policy documents, they reflect the development policy of the government over time. For this reason, their provisions are still worth considering in the discussion of the domestic framework.

The NGP embodies Zambia's vision as regards gender. One of the primary aims of the policy is to reduce gender imbalances such as gender disparities in positions of decision-making. The NGP provides guidelines for addressing barriers that prevent equal and effective participation of men and women in national development.[30] The NGP responds to the observed trend that women have been deprived from decision-making positions. The provisions in the most recent national development plan are couched to work hand in hand with the NGP.

Published every five years, Zambia's national development plans embody the government's development agenda. Each plan narrates the past performance of government in various areas of national and economic interest[31] and provide the strategies government plans to employ to achieve the development outcomes.

The private sector and civil society could use the contents of these plans. The plans can be used to sensitize the general populace and develop ways to hold governments more accountable. Investors can also gain further clarity regarding the social and economic goals to be met by investments in the country over the five-year period covered by the plans.

Zambia is currently on its seventh national development plan set over a five-year period starting in 2017. The 7NDP's provisions are worth exploring as they present a picture of the most recent strategies government plans to employ.

27 Available at https://extranet.sadc.int/files/2112/9794/9109/SADC_PROTOCOL_ON_GENDER_AND_DEVELOPMENT.pdf.

28 GEEA, s 1.

29 Act No. 10 of 2019.

30 Ministry of Gender and Child Development, Program for the protection and promotion women and child rights in Zambia Program Document 16th July 2012.

31 Examples include Agriculture, Mining, Education and Health.

The 7NDP lists reducing developmental inequalities among Zambia's development outcomes. Addressing gender inequality is cited as one of the strategies in this regard.[32]

The 7NDP states that addressing gender inequality remains an important issue for policy in Zambia. This is placed into the context of the SDG number 5 which is aimed at providing women and girls with equal access to education, health care, decent work and representation in political and economic decision-making processes. The State has indicated that achieving this Goal will be the Government's focus during the 7NDP's five-year period.

As a source of policy direction regarding investment and gender, the 7NDP is helpful in at least two respects. First, the Plant's Development Outcomes guide investor's as to what priority areas the government will be focussing on and, in turn, is likely legislate upon. Second, and more importantly, the strategies included in the Plan provide an accountability mechanism upon which government actions can be assessed during and after the five year period.

In the period since the publication of the 7NDP, mechanisms such as the affirmative action plan have yet to be realized. However, this can be attributed to the status of the enactment of the Gender Equity and Equality Act[33] which is to serve as Zambia's principal legislation.

To gain a fuller understanding of gender aspects of investment law, reference must also be made to international instruments. These directly impacted the formulation of the domestic gender policy.

5.3.2 International sources of law

Zambia's obligations stem from international obligation which are applicable at global level and regional level. At global level, Zambia is signatory to the Convention on the Elimination of all forms of Discrimination against Women (**"CEDAW"**) and the United Nations Fourth World Conference on Women of 1995 (**"the Beijing Platform"**). Similar to the CEDAW and Beijing Platform, Zambia among twelve Countries signed the Declaration on Gender and Development (**"the Declaration"**) in the Southern Region of Africa.[34]

5.3.2.1 Global instruments

Adopted by the United Nations General Assembly in 1979, the CEDAW provided the basis of realizing gender equality between women and men, as it gives an international prohibition of gender discrimination. Zambia signed the CEDAW in 1980 and ratified it in 1985; committing to undertaking a series of measures to end discrimination against women.[35]

32 7NDP, Para 9.3.3.
33 Act No. 22 of 2015.
34 SADC Declaration on Gender and Development (1997).
35 See also the International Covenant on Civil and Political Rights which prohibits discrimination on the basis of gender.

Similarly, the Beijing Platform aims to realize gender equality in all spheres of life. The Beijing Platform recognizes the considerable difference in women and men's access to and opportunities to exert power over economies in their societies.[36] As a result, the Beijing Platform seeks to promote and protect the full enjoyment of all human rights and fundamental freedoms of women. The purpose of the Beijing Platform mitigates factors influencing women's participation in the mining sector. As the Beijing Platform require immediate action by State to promote and protect women's human rights. This include; rights to education, economic resources and protection against discrimination. Further the platform for Action upholds the CEDAW and believes that a transformed partnership based on equality between women and men is a condition for people-centred sustainable development.[37]

5.3.2.2 Regional instruments

At regional level, the Declaration reaffirms SADC's commitment to eliminating gender discrimination and mainstreaming gender issues in Southern Africa.[38] Further, in 2008, the SADC Heads of State signed and adopted the SADC Protocol on Gender and Development.[39] The objectives of the protocol, as set out in Article 3 provide for the empowerment of women, elimination of discrimination and to achieve gender equality. The Protocol is a step to harmonize the various international, continental and regional gender equality instruments that SADC has subscribed to such as: CEDAW, Beijing Declaration From the domestic and international source, certain themes and obligations can be drawn out.

5.4 Themes and obligations in the gender and investment framework

The framework for gender and investment comprises complex sources from which numerous themes and obligation can be discussed. The discussion here is limited to a selection based on the themes and obligations with the most potential impact on investment in Zambia. The themes which arise from the framework are related to the achievement of gender equity, equality, and empowerment as objectives in the framework. These objectives are set out before discussing the State's obligations to protect, promote and regulate investment. The discussion concludes with a discussion of the obligations with which investors must comply with in pursuit of gender equity, equality and the empowerment of women in Zambia. The final area of concern is dispute resolution as changes in policy can lead to investor-State disputes.

36 "The United Nations Fourth World Conference on Women". *Action for Equality, Development and Peace* (Beijing 1995) http://www.un.org/womenwatch/daw/beijing/platform/.

37 Ibid.

38 See also Article 18(3) of the African Charter of Human and Peoples' Rights.

39 http://www.sadc.int/issues/gender/.org.

5.4.1 Gender equity, equality and empowerment as objectives in the legal frameworks

The legal framework has given a particular umbrella to themes of "gender equity", "gender equality" and "empowerment". As the supreme law of Zambia, The Constitution's[40] provision provides a starting point for enactment of all provisions relating to gender and investment. Article 23 provides for protection against all forms of discrimination. The provisions of the GEEA and the obligations on the investors and the government are to be read in light of this provision.

The GEEA provides definitions of the terms "discrimination", "equality", "equity" and "empower" in section 2. Each of these basic principles in gender discourse. The definition of discrimination read:

> a distinction, exclusion or restriction made on the basis of sex or any other ground which has the effect or purpose of impairing or nullifying the dignity of a person or the recognition, enjoyment or exercise by a person of that person's rights and freedoms as specified in the Constitution or any other law.

Section 15 of the GEEA explicitly prohibits discrimination on grounds of sex. This provision consolidates both the international[41] and Zambia's Constitutional protections provided to women. The definition of equality reads:

> the full and equal enjoyment, by both sexes, of rights, opportunities, responsibilities and freedoms, and where both sexes are equally treated, in accordance with the Constitution and this Act.
>
> This definition is to be compared with the definition of equity which is defined as "the just and fair distribution of benefits, rewards and opportunities between both sexes".

Though related, these two aims are not the same[42] and the GEEA clearly sets that out. Investors are thus required to take note of this distinction as they develop an understanding of the obligations imposed under the GEEA. The term empower and, the related term, empowerment are defined in the GEEA as, "[gaining] access to opportunities and develop a person's capacities so as to shape that person's life or that of the person's community, in all spheres of life".

The GEEA lists the guiding principles for the achievement of gender equity and equality in section 4. Among these are "*the empowerment of women as a key to achieving gender equity and equality*"[43] and a cooperation between

40 The Constitution of Zambia. Chapter one of the Laws of Zambia.

41 See CEDAW, Article 1; Maputo Protocol, Article 2 and SADC Protocol, Article 6(1).

42 See Sohela Nazneen, Sam Hickey and Eleni Sifaki (eds.), *Negotiating Gender Equity in the Global South: The Politics of Domestic Violence Policy* (Routledge 2019).

43 GEEA, section 4(e).

the public and private sector.[44] Section 23 empowers the Minister of Gender to develop policies and drive development of further legislation in pursuit of the GEEA's objectives. Investors are thus required to participate in providing access and opportunities through the businesses they operate in Zambia. The above definitions and principles are crafted to reflect the principles set out in the CEDAW. Thus, investors are to refer to the CEDAW and the interpretation given to them by the United Nations' Committee on the Elimination of Discrimination against Women which monitors the application of these principles.[45]

From a policy perspective, the 7NDP, the strategy is to reduce the gender gap by "*structural impediments which perpetuate gender inequality in the country*".[46] The said "structural impediments" are not defined in the plan. However, the State confesses an awareness that there are unbalanced power relations between women and men in the domestic, community and public domains remain impediments to the advancement of women.[47] The State further confesses that Zambian women have fewer decision-making positions compared to men at all levels and remain the worst victims of the country's high unemployment and poverty.[48] This impediment can be observed from the fact that women are underrepresented in Zambia's legislature,[49] judiciary and cabinet. This is despite the nation having a female Deputy-Speaker of the National Assembly,[50] Chief Justice and Vice President.[51]

From an economic perspective, the 7NDP records that women have differentiated access to credit, improved technology, land and extension services.[52] Each of these issues constrains agricultural productivity and other economic activities.[53] It is thus expected that the government has an obligation to address these issues as priority issues in regulation of investment. The mechanisms set to address gender inequality are "collaboration and use of a holistic multi-sectoral approach" to promote women's economic empowerment programmes "affirmative action for women, gender mainstreaming and promotion of girl child education".[54] No particulars are given as to what each mechanism will entail. However, given the general nature of the Development Outcomes and corresponding strategies given in the 7NDP, this is to be expected.

44 Ibid.
45 See https://www.ohchr.org/en/professionalinterest/pages/cedaw.aspx.
46 7NDP, Para 9.3.3.
47 Ibid.
48 Ibid.
49 It is reported that women represent 18.1% of the legislature. See http://www.parliament.gov.zm/members/gender.
50 See profile of Honourable Catherine Namugala M.P. at http://www.parliament.gov.zm/node/370.
51 See profile for Her Honour Inonge Wina at https://www.ovp.gov.zm/.
52 7NDP, Para 9.3.3.
53 Ibid.
54 Ibid.

The above principles and protections are to be enforced through the institutional arrangements the put in place by the GEEA.

5.4.2 Obligations on the State and investors regarding gender and investment

Obligations introduced in the pursuit of gender parity have effects on both the host State and the investor. The host State is required not only to develop regulation but also enforce policy through relevant government institution. As such, the institutions established for the enforcement of gender legislation are to be closely examined. For investors, developments in gender policy may introduce new obligations or provide opportunities for new ways of doing business using the "shared value" model of doing business. Analogy can be drawn from the manner in which environmental policy has been introduced in Zambia.

Having ratified various international instruments for the protection of the environment,[55] Zambia has passed a various legislation[56] in observance of her obligations thereunder. Numerous institutions[57] have been developed in pursuit of these obligations and to ensure that persons and companies operating in the country are compliant with environmental legislation. Investors are expected to become more and more aware of the importance of compliance in this regard. As such, they should watch policy changes to environmental policy more and more closely. Gender policy, equally should be of concern.

Reaction to recent changes in gender legislation have shown how sensitive the private sector is to gender issues. Some companies, particularly in the financial services sector, have also developed their business practices to address the unique needs of women in order to develop a more inclusive consumer base.[58] Even without a direct cause-and-effect relationship between gender policy and private sector business strategy; gender issues present a business case to be address by both regulators of and participants in investment.

The discourse about investment law and policy here is focussed first on the broader State obligation to protect, promote and regulate investments and the State institutions established to enforce international obligations regarding gender. Only after the State's obligations are clearly set out should investors' obligation be discussed.

55 For example the Rio Declaration, 1992 and Paris Convention, 1983.

56 For example Environmental Management Act No. 12 of 2011; Water Resources Management No. 21 of 2011; Zambia Wildlife Act No. 14 of 2015.

57 I.e. the Zambia Environmental Management Agency, Water Resources Management Authority and the Department of National Parks and Wildlife.

58 For example two of the biggest financial institutions, Stanbic Bank and Access Bank, have each developed baking products uniquely designed for women namely "Anakadzi Banking" and the "W Initiative" respectively. See https://anakazibanking.com and https://zambia.accessbank-plc.com/pages/sustainable-banking/Our-Community-Investments/Community-Support/The-W%E2%80%9D-Initiative.aspx.

5.4.3 State obligations to protect, promote and regulate investment

The State obligation to protect investments stems from the Bill of Rights in Part III of the Constitution. It is from the Bill of Rights that all investments, whether owned by local and foreign, can glean the protections over their property rights. Article 16(1) provides:

> Except as provided in this Article, no property of any description shall be compulsorily taken possession of, and no interest in or right over property of any description shall be compulsorily acquired, unless by or under the authority of an Act of Parliament which provides for payment of adequate compensation for the property or interest or right to be taken possession of or acquired.

Article 16 of the Constitution is the empowering provision under which the Lands Acquisition Act[59] was enacted. The stated purpose of this Act according to its Preamble is *"to make provision for the compulsory acquisition of land and other property"*. This Preamble extends the scope of the Act beyond immovable property (as its name suggests) and makes the Act applicable to the expropriation of moveable property such as shares. The whole Act is dedicated to determining how and when expropriation can take place. Key provision as regards expropriation include the empowering and procedural provisions which are housed in Part II (sections 3–9). The provisions of this Act are supplemented by the provisions of the Zambia Development Agency Act. Section 19(1) of the ZDA Act provides:

> An investor's property shall not be compulsorily acquired nor shall any interest in or right over such property be compulsorily acquired except for public purposes under an Act of Parliament relating to the compulsory acquisition of property which provides for payment of compensation for such acquisition.

The above provision uses the term "public purpose" which is not defined in the legislation. This has made the term a subject of judicial interpretation. The judicial interpretation of this term can be taken from contrasting at least two key decisions of the Supreme Court of Zambia on this matter. The first decision is that of *Wise v. the Attorney General.*[60] In this matter, the Appellant was a foreign national had inherited land which was being leased out for farming purposes to a private company. The Appellant decided to terminate the leases much to the chagrin of the owners of the lessee company who were, as the Appellant came to learn, well politically connected. In a turn of events that saw government

59 Chapter 189 of the Laws of Zambia.
60 (1990/92) ZR 124.

officials intervening in the Appellant's exercise of his property rights through meeting to try and convince him to carry on the lease, the Appellant's land was expropriated and he was summarily deported. In its decision on the matter, the Supreme Court laid down the following points regarding how to determine whether the government's action was done for a public purpose. First, the Court stated that the purpose depends on the circumstances of the particular case. Second, because the State did not disclose the public purpose for which the land was compulsorily acquired, the Court held that the public interest was too remote and there was no immediate need to acquire the farms. Finally, as to the question of whether the government exercised its power of acquisition in *mala fides*, the Court considered the circumstances surrounding the compulsory acquisition. The court found that the acquisition was done in bad faith. The Court nullified the expropriation; awarding damages to the Appellant.

Three factors were considered in the *Wise* case namely the circumstances of the case, the purpose for the expropriation and the mala fides or bona fides of the government's action. Taking these together could guide one to determine whether the expropriation was for a public purpose. The second case to consider in this regard is the case of *Zambia National Holdings Limited and United National Independence Party (UNIP) v. The Attorney-General.*[61] In this matter, the newly elected government of the Movement for Multi-party Democracy (MMD) party expropriated the national headquarters of the previously ruling UNIP. This expropriation was challenged and the litigation went up to the Supreme Court. The Court was called upon to consider the purpose for the expropriation and the mala fides of the government's action. In its decision, the Court considered the circumstances of the case. The expropriation was upheld on the basis that the MMD government had stated that the purpose for taking the property was to recover public funds used to construct the building which was for private use.

The Zambian framework also provides the State with an obligation to create investment promotion measures. The mechanism in place is through various incentives. The term "incentive" refers to legal mechanisms to encourage investment in general. As was seen, double tax agreements serve as an incentive.[62] Tax and customs exemption are generally considered the main form in which incentives are given.[63] However incentives can take other forms.

One such example is the freedom to transfer and deal in foreign currency. Because many companies operating in foreign countries may prefer to trade in widely traded currencies such as the United States Dollar, the ability to easily trade in such currencies encourages investment. The imposition of currency control in the law in form of exchange control provisions can tend to deter international investors. The ZDA Act provides a host of incentives in section 20 and Part 8.

61 (1994) S.J. 22

62 ZDA Act, Part 8.

63 Kenneth Kaoma Mwenda, "Legal Aspects of Foreign Direct Investment in Zambia" (1999) 6 *Murdoch University Electronic Journal of Law* 35–51 at 38–39.

Section 20 provides that for externalization of funds whereby a foreign investor may transfer out of Zambia in foreign currency after payment of the relevant taxes. This acts as an incentive for any investors who may worry about exchange controls or other estrictions on the repatriation of their money out of Zambia.

Part 8 is dedicated to incentives which are to be designed and determined by The Minister of Finance shall in consultation with the Minister of Commerce.[64] Incentives offered under ZDA Act is valid for five years from the grant of the licence, permit or certificate or for such period as the Minister responsible for finance may prescribe.[65]

To qualify for incentives must invest a certain amount of money. An investor investing not less than five hundred thousand United States Dollars in a priority sector[66] or product is entitled to tax incentives.[67] There is also tax exemption for machinery or equipment for operations in a priority sector or in respect of priority products; or a rural enterprise.[68] An investor must hold a license, permit or certificate of registration to qualify to incentives.[69]

Section 61 provides for Double taxation agreements whereby if a double taxation agreement exists, between Zambia and another country, foreign tax payable by an investor to the other country in respect of any foreign income shall be as determined under that agreement. To promote infrastructure development, incentives are also provided in relation to bonded factories and warehouses.[70]

The State has put in place these and other incentives as an investment-attraction measure. The aim of these measures has been to attract foreign direct investment and this Zambia has done successfully.[71] What is not seen in these incentives is the impact these incentives have on domestic investors in general and, in particular, domestic investors who are women.

In meeting its obligations to regulate modern investments, the State must look into investigating the extent to which women are benefitting from existing incentives. The State is further invited to develop the existing incentives in order that investments can assist to achieve the aims of the GEEA whenever that Act comes into force. The development of incentives in this will also assist in the State meeting its obligation to enforce gender law and policy.

64 ZDA Act, Section 54.

65 ZDA Act, Section 55.

66 Priority Sectors are listed in the Second Schedule of the ZDA Act and these include Floriculture, Horticulture, Processed foods, Beverages and stimulants, manufacturing of copper products and production of leather products.

67 ZDA Act, Section 56.

68 ZDA Act, Section 57.

69 ZDA Act, Section 59.

70 ZDA Act, Sections 62 and 63.

71 See *Zambia Development Agency 2016–2020 Strategic Plan: Transforming business for the benefit of Zambians* (2016) 19.

5.4.4 State obligations to enforce gender law and policy

In response to the aims set out by the Beijing Platform, the Ministry of Gender and Child Development in the year 2014, presented a report on the implementation of the Beijing Platform in Zambia. The report reveals steps taken by Zambian government towards the implementation of the Beijing Platform. The Ministry of Gender and Child Development among others listed the following achievements on the implementation of the Beijing Platform[72]:

- Creation of the Ministry of Gender and Child Development in 2012 to oversee gender mainstreaming and empowerment of women in both public and private sectors.
- The creation of Economic Empowerment Fund for women by Government and
- Formulation and adoption of the National Gender policy in 2000 and its implementation in 2004.

These achievements by the State are measures to mitigate factors that contribute to the low participation levels of women in the Zambia economy. Through then Ministry of Gender and Child Development, the State monitors the process of gender mainstreaming in the different economic sectors. Gender mainstreaming involves the integration of a gender perspective into the preparation, implementation, monitoring and evaluation of policies and regulatory measures. All this is done with a view to promoting equality between women and men and combating discrimination.[73]

The GEEA provides institutional arrangements and obligations which are noteworthy to both investors and the society in the host State. The GEEA provides certain key principles from which investors' obligations can be developed. The Act also establishes some key institutions which would guide investors on how they could aid in the State's efforts to achieve its gender-related objectives.

The GEEA places the primary responsibility for implementation of the GEEA on the Minister of Gender.[74] In this regard the Minister is empowered to pass a statutory instrument for the Act to come into operation.[75] As at the date of authoring this publication, however, no such instrument has been passed. This is attributable to the onerous obligations which the State would have to put in place to enforce the GEEA.

72 Ministry Gender and Child Development. *Zambia Progress Report On The Implementation Of The Beijing Declaration And Platform Of Action (1995) And The Outcome Of The Twenty-Third Special Session Of The General Assembly (2000)*, (2014).

73 http://www.un.org/gendermainstreaming.htm.

74 GEEA, s5(1).

75 GEEA, s 1.

The GEEA establishes the Gender Equity and Equality Commission to support the work of the Ministry of Gender.[76] This Commission has wide powers to monitor the implementation of the GEEAs and advise various ministries and agencies on gender issues.[77] The powers of the Commission are designed to ensure prohibition of discrimination on basis sex.[78] The GEEA also provides that gender equality is practiced in both public[79] and private[80] institutions; both of which would be subject to the powers of the Commission.

Due to the far-reaching powers of the Commission created by the GEEA, the protections and entitlements the Act provides to women would be relevant in the context of investment. A key provision in this regard is the requirement that both men and women should be given equal opportunity to decision-making positions.[81] The enforcement of such a provision would require that the Commission put measures to encourage women to take up leadership positions in the private or public sectors. Among the provision to facilitate this process is a mechanism progressive realization towards 50% representation and meaningful participation of women.[82] Such is the progressive nature of the GEEA's provisions

The private sector is expected to actively participate in achieving the stated goals of the Act. Non-compliance with the Act may result in the investor receiving a directive[83] or compliance notice[84] from the Minister of Gender. There is also provision for searches with[85] or without[86] warrant to investigate compliance with the Act. The Act also provides for criminal penalties to be imposed for non-compliance with the Act,[87] penalties which can also be extended to persons in the public sector.

The financial implications of setting up the Commission in light of other obligations to which the Ministry of Gender should adhere under the Act could justify why the GEEA has yet to be brought into effect.[88] This can be inferred from the rights extended to women which the Commission would have the power to enforce. Further, the widely crafted institutional arrangements and enforcement mechanisms in the GEEA give the Act the potential of radically changing the regulation of investment in Zambia. For this reason, investors would be well advised to take note of its provision ahead of its entry into force.

76 GEEA, s6.
77 GEEA, s9(1)(a)-(d).
78 GEEA, s9(2)(a)-(c).
79 GEEA, s17, 18.
80 GEEA, s17, 18.
81 GEEA, s 24.
82 Section 24 (d) of the Gender Equity and Equality Act [No. 22 of 2015].
83 GEEA, s 47(1).
84 GEEA, s 48(1).
85 GEEA, s 50.
86 GEEA, s 49.
87 GEEA, s 56.
88 Country Gender Profile: Zambia Final Report March 2016 Japan International Cooperation Agency (JICA) Japan Development Service Co., Ltd. (JDS).

Under the NGP, the government seeks to ensure that women participation in increased in decision-making positions at all levels in both the public and private sectors of the country. Under 5.5 (b) (i) and (ii) there is talk about how this will be done. Advocate for increased participation of women in decision-making through undertaking sensitization campaigns for women to participate in decision-making and lobby for women's participation with selected stake holders through meetings, letters, press statements, focussed group discussions and role modelling.[89] The National Gender Policy[90] plays an important role in this research as it shows the vision of the country with regards its gender policy.

5.4.5 Investor obligations towards achieving gender equity

The Gender Equity and Equality Act, creates various obligations for investors. For example, section 18(1) requires private bodies to "develop equity and equality plans, codes of practice, regulatory mechanisms and other appropriate measures for the effective promotion of gender equity and equality in the area of its operation". They must also enforce and monitor these and also make regular reports to the Ministry of Gender, the Commission and any other relevant monitoring bodies. Section 18(2) goes further to say that, "The Minister shall, by statutory instrument, make regulations on the development and implementation of, and reporting on, equity and equality plans and codes of practice by private bodies, in a manner proportionate to a private body's size, resources and influence".

Section 19 also imposes obligations on both public and private bodies. Section 19(1) places an obligation on all these bodies. They are expected to do this by inter alia:

- changing the conditions and circumstances which hinder achievement of sustainable and substantive gender equity and equality;
- mainstreaming gender in all "strategies, policies, programmes and budgets" in order to empower and benefit both sexes;
- ensuring accommodation of the needs and interests of both sexes;
- establishing appropriate and special measures which are designed to recognize and support the multiple roles of women.

In addition, under section 19(1)(e) public and private bodies also have the role of enforcing gender equity and equality legislation, policies and strategies. It is prescribed that they do this through setting targets to improve compliance with such legislation, policies and strategies. They should also audit any factors that contribute to non-compliance. In addition to this, they are to encourage and reward compliance with such legislation, policies and strategies. They can also ensure compliance by implementing appropriate corrective measures if needed.

89 Ibid.
90 Ibid.

Section 27(1) prohibits the discrimination against women in social and economic life. This involves ensuring the full development and advancement of women on an equal basis with men. Moreover, under section 31, a woman is to have "on the equal basis with a man" the same access to employment opportunities. This includes inter alia "equal remuneration, benefits and treatment in respect of work of equal value as well as equality of treatment in the evaluation of the quality of work". Failure to abide by this attracts a fine or to imprisonment or both.

Another Act that creates obligations for investors and private entities is the Employment Code Act. Enacted in 2019, the Employment Code[91] introduced some radical changes to the face of Zambian labour law in general and gender and investment in particular. The provisions with the highest potential impact on investment and gender are found among the Code's Minimum Employee Benefits. These benefits represent the bare minimum benefits a female employee can expect under an employment contract. Some of the protections provided to female employees can be altered by agreement between employee and employer.

Female employees are entitled to one day's absence from work each month without having to produce a medical certificate or give reason to the employer.[92] This section provides for what is colloquially known as "Mother's day" and is one of the progressive provisions in the- Code as regards recognizing the unique needs of women in the workforce

Section 41 which provides for Maternity leave has introduced some of the most radical changes in the Code. This section grants fourteen weeks maternity leave to female employees.[93] The employee is entitled to a further four weeks in case of a multiple birth.[94] The term can also be extended on the recommendation of a medical doctor for a woman who gives birth to a premature child.[95] A female employee who suffers a miscarriage during the third trimester of pregnancy or bears a still born child is entitled to six weeks leave on full pay immediately after the miscarriage or still birth.[96] The section grants full pay to an employee for the period of maternity leave provided she has been employed for a 24 months prior to taking maternity leave.[97] Upon the end of maternity leave, a female employee is guaranteed to return to the job she held immediately before the maternity leave or another job on terms and conditions not less favourable than the job held before the maternity leave. [98] The employer can reclaim the salary paid to the employee from a third party benefit scheme where such scheme is in place.[99] The employee will not forfeit any other leave days to which she may be entitled

91 Act No. 10 of 2019.

92 Employment Code, Section 47.

93 Section 41(1).

94 Section 41(2).

95 Section 41(5). In this section, "premature child" means a child born before thirty-seven weeks of gestation counting from the first day of the last menstrual cycle. See section 41(11).

96 Section 41(6).

97 Section 41(3).

98 Section 41(7).

99 Section 41(4).

just because she took maternity leave.[100] If need be, a female employee may go on other categories of leaves such as sick, annual or compassionate leave immediately after taking maternity leave.[101] All the protection afforded by section 41 can be only be altered by an investor granting more favourable conditions to the employee.[102]

Section 42 requires that before she returns to work after maternity leave, a female employee's fitness to resume work must be certified by a medical doctor. Section 43 protects employees from being against dismissed for reasons connected with pregnancy or maternity leave. The Employment Code would only allow dismissal for reasons such as gross misconduct, habitual or substantial neglect of the employee's duties, and continual absence from work without the permission or breach of disciplinary rules.[103]

Section 44 provides a number of obligations for employers to protect female employees from harmful work. What qualifies as "harmful work" under this section is to for an employer to require a female employee to perform work in excess of a normal day's work, two months before her estimated date of delivery.[104] Harmful work can also include requiring a pregnant employee to do work which involves continuous standing or other work which may be detrimental to the employee or the unborn child.[105] The employer has an obligation to offer the employee suitable alternative employment, if practicable, on terms and conditions that are not less favourable than that employee's terms and conditions of employment.[106] There is also an obligation for an employer to exempt a pregnant or nursing employee from working at night.[107]

Employers also have obligations that extend after the employee has given birth. Section 45 provides that an employee is entitled to take two nursing breaks of thirty minutes each; or one nursing break of one hour of at a time convenient to the employee and having regard to the needs of the child.[108] The employer is to allow such nursing breaks for a period of six months from the date of delivery and may not be deducted from the number of paid hours of work of that female employee.[109] This protection can be altered by agreement between employer and employee on terms which are more favourable than the provisions of section 45.[110]

The Employment Code also provides protection for male employees in this regard. Section 46 provides that a male employee is entitled to take at least five continuous working days as paternity leave; which leave is to be taken within

100 Section 41(8).
101 Ibid.
102 Section 41(10).
103 Section 50 (1).
104 Section 44(1).
105 Section 44(2)(a)–(b).
106 Section 44(3).
107 Section 44(4).
108 Section 45(1).
109 Section 45(2).
110 Section 45(3).

seven days of the birth of a child. To take such leave, the employee must be the father of the child and has submit a birth record of the child to the employer.[111]

Section 127 provides that where there are more favourable conditions and terms in an employment contract, collective agreement or legislation, such conditions will prevail over the provisions of the Employment Code.

These Minimum Employee Benefits show a legislated commitment by Zambia's government to achieving gender equity and equality. By providing these seemingly onerous obligations to employers, the government has opened up the possibility that female employees may not be a preferred choice during selection for employment. However, given the constitutional protection against discrimination, any employer or investor who may not easily avoid the obligations in the Employment Code as they would run the risk of being sued.

What remains to be seen is how these provisions are to be implemented by investors employing female employees. As such, the relevance of the development outcomes and legal obligations towards achieving gender equity and equality must be monitored over time. In this regard, reference must be made to the dispute settlement mechanisms in the legal framework in case gender issues form the subject of investor-State disputes.

5.4.6 Settlement of investor-state disputes

The possibility of investor-State disputes arising from changes in policy is ever-present. Detailed discussion of such disputes is outside the scope of this chapter but citing a few examples provides a suitable starting point for an exploration of the mechanisms provided in the legal framework for investment.

Investor-State disputes can arise from various sources and among these is the breach or perceived breach of obligations on the part of the host State. These obligations can be found in national legislation[112] or in agreements entered between States or agreements. For this chapter, legislated obligations are the focus as these form part of the general policy framework for investment.

In some investor-State disputes, a change in government policy can directly lead to an investment dispute.[113] The host government can make policy changes in the interest of what was deemed good for the nation. This was true of policy shifts in Libya in the 1970s as regards the nationalization of the nation's oil fields[114] and Zimbabwe in the 2000s in nationalization of agricultural land.[115]

It is therefore possible that "good" changes in public policy can lead to investment disputes. As such, progressive changes towards addressing gender

111 Section 46.

112 For example, the Zambian Constitution in Article 16 creates an obligation for the state not to deprive persons of their property. This protection is repeated in section 19 of the Zambia Development Agency Act (Zambia's principal investment legislation) and the Lands Acquisition Act Chapter 189 of the Laws of Zambia (Zambia's principal expropriation legislation).

113 For example *LIAMCO v Libya Award* 12 April 1977.

114 Sangwani Patrick Ng'ambi, *Understanding Investment Law in Zambia* (Juta 2016) 60.

115 *Mike Campbell and Others v Zimbabwe* SADC (T) Case No. 2/2007.

inequality can have the indirect and unintended consequence of causing investment disputes. Illustration of this can be drawn from the *Decision on Jurisdiction Enron Corporation and Ponderosa Assets, L.P v The Argentine Republic.*[116]

The facts of the *Enron* case serve as an example of how an investment dispute can arise indirectly from changes in public policy.

The investments which formed the subject of the dispute were made by the Claimants during the privatization of the gas industry of Argentina which commenced in 1989.[117] The Claimants had been invited by the Argentine Government to participate in the privatization programme through various incentives.[118] The change in public policy which led to the Claimants resorting arbitration at the International Centre for Settlement of Investment Disputes (**"ICSID"**) was in relation to the taxation of the gas industry.

The governments of Argentina and the United States entered a Bilateral Investment Treaty (**"BIT"**) which guaranteed that taxes on the gas industry would be set at federal level by the Argentine government; which taxes would take into account the price index set in the United States. However, after a change of government in the 2000s, the Argentine government allowed for taxes to be set by the respective provinces in which the Claimants gas operations were located. This imposition of different taxes was considered by the Claimants to be a breach of the BIT.

Before commencing the trial at ICSID, The Claimants first had to confirm the jurisdiction of the ICSID Tribunal. The Argentine government raised a jurisdictional objection due to the lack of direct connection to the investment.[119] It was argued that the Claimants' concerns involved individual tax assessments which had nothing to do with the BIT in question.

In confirming its jurisdiction, the Tribunal reasoned that the Claimants had a cause of action due to the invest protection afforded by the Argentina-United States BIT; which protection was threatened by the change in national policy. Thus, a change in tax policy became a source of an investment dispute within the jurisdiction of ICSID even though it may have appeared that the connection was remote.

Like changes to tax policy, changes to gender policy should be considered a cause concern for investors. This is because changes to gender policy are likely to cause investor-State disputes where the investment has a bearing of human rights. The case *Velasquez Rodriguez v Honduras*[120] illustrates this point. In that case, it was held that a State has a positive duty to prevent human rights violations occurring in its territory. By implication, States must protect victims from discrimination even from private investors.[121]

116 ICSID Case No. Arb/01/3.
117 Para 50.
118 Para 52.
119 Para 54.
120 Inter-Am.Ct.H.R. (Ser. C) No. 4 (1988).
121 See also *Sara H. Longwe v Intercontinental Hotels* 1992/HP/765 (1993) 4 LRC 221.

In Zambia, Dispute resolution is provided for in the Lands Acquisition Act and the ZDA Act. Section 11 of the Lands Acquisition Act provides for disputes regarding compensation to be referred to court by litigation. Section 21 of the ZDA Act provides for settlement of disputes "*arising as a consequence of an investment under this Act*" to be settled by arbitration.[122]

It can be observed that a change in *government* and the resultant change in policy have been the source of investment disputes. This was illustrated in the case of *Zambia National Holdings and Another v the Attorney-General.*[123]

The dispute in *Zambia National Holdings* case arose because a new government took over in 1991 and nationalized a building which served as the political party headquarters of the previous government; which building was owned by the Appellants in the matter. The main legal question in the matter was whether the nationalization was done in good faith and in the public interest. The Zambian Supreme Court reasoned that the nationalization was in the public interest because public funds had been used to acquire the building in question.

A question regarding the operation of section 11 arose in the *Zambia National Holdings* case. It was argued by the Appellants that section 11(4) suggests that the government must make an upfront payment for expropriated property. However, the Court clarified that the prerequisite for such payment is a dispute about the quantum of compensation payable. As such, it is not a blanket requirement that compensation be paid upfront.

What is seen from the above case is that property rights can be interrupted in the public interest. As previously stated, the pursuit of gender equality is likely to cause an indirect interruption to investments due to the introduction of new rights for citizens of a host State and imposition of new obligations on the investor. For this reason, the policy and legislative provisions impose obligations on investors must be explored.

5.5 Implications of the stabilization clauses in concession agreements

As highlighted, the copper industry in Zambia underwent three phases. It was first in the hands of private companies, namely Anglo-American Corporation and the Roan Selection Trust.[124] These were eventually nationalized to form ZCCM.[125] When ZCCM began to operate at a loss, the government of Zambia was pressurized into privatizing the said entity. To foster the process of

122 "Investment" is defined in section 2 as a contribution of capital, in cash or in kind, by an investor to a new business enterprise, to the expansion or rehabilitation of an existing business enterprise or to the purchase of an existing business enterprise from the State. As will be seen in Unit Four, this definition provides a wide scope of application for the arbitration of disputes under the domestic framework.

123 (1993/94) ZR 115 (SC).

124 Sangwani Patrick Ng'ambi, *Resource Nationalism in International Investment Law* (Routledge 2016) 114.

125 Ibid.

privatization, the government entered into a number of development agreements with foreign mining companies. These development agreements were facilitated through the Mines and Minerals Act 1995.[126] Development agreements were defined in the Mines and Minerals Act of 1995 as "an agreement entered into under section nine in relation to a large-scale mining license". Section 9(1) of the said Act states as follows:

> 9 (1) For the purpose of encouraging and protecting large-scale investments in the mining sector in Zambia, the Minister may, on behalf of the Republic, enter into an agreement relating to the grant of a large-scale mining license.
> (2) An agreement referred to in subsection (1) shall be known as a development agreement, and may contain provisions, which notwithstanding the provisions of any law or regulation shall be binding on the Republic ...

Thus, the Minister was granted the authority by an Act of Parliament, to enter into development agreements, with foreign mining companies. In addition to this, the provisions of the contract were also binding on the government of the Republic of Zambia. All of the Development agreements generally contained tax stability clauses. In addition, some of them contained general stabilization clauses, in addition to tax stability clauses. An example of the wording of the general stabilization clause is contained in the Development Agreement with Konkola Copper Mines. It stated as follows:

> GRZ further undertakes, during the Stability Period, it shall not by general or special legislation or by administrative measures or decree or by any other action or omission whatsoever (other than an act of nationalisation such as is referred to in Clause 0) ("GRZ Action") vary, amend, cancel or terminate this Agreement or the rights and obligations of the Parties under this Agreement, or cause this Agreement or the said rights and obligations to be varied, amended, cancelled or terminated, or prevent or hinder performance of this Agreement by any party thereto, provided always that this Agreement and the rights and obligations of the Parties under this Agreement may be varied, amended, cancelled or terminated as expressly provided herein. GRZ undertakes that KCM and its officers, directors, employees and shareholders shall be held free and made exempt from any GRZ Action or any change in the law of Zambia which would, but for such freedom or exemption, adversely affect KCM's rights under, or KCM's ability to comply with its obligations under, this Agreement.

The tax stability clauses in the contracts were more specific. Under these agreements, the government promised not to increase taxes, including corporate tax and royalties for a stability period of fifteen to twenty years, in a way that would have a "material adverse effect" on the distributable profits of the foreign-owned

126 Chapter 218 of the Laws of Zambia (now repealed).

mining companies.[127] These clauses essentially sought to preclude the government from increasing taxes and introducing any new taxes for the tax stability period stipulated in the development agreements.[128]

There is much speculation as to why the Zambian government entered into such asymmetrical agreements in the first place.[129] The answer lies in the fact that Zambia was trying to attract foreign direct investment, into a sector that was making losses at the time, due to low copper prices on the LME. Because of the low copper prices, it should come as no surprise that foreign mining companies were not particularly enthusiastic about investing in Zambia. The government was thus left in the precarious position of providing tax incentives or simply closing the mines.[130] According to Edith Nawakwi, who is former Minister of Finance, the mines at the time were making losses of up to one million dollars a day. In order to pay salaries to mineworkers, the government were forced to borrow large sums. In addition, the government of Zambia would have needed to raise huge sums of money to resuscitate the mining industry. The government was in no position to do this. For this reason, the government had to attract foreign direct investment in order to raise the necessary capital. In order to do that, they would have to accept the terms of those who did wish to investment in Zambia, pernicious as those terms seemed. Moreover, the government was also under pressure from the World Bank and the IMF to privatize the mines, in order for Zambia to qualify for debt relief. To borrow the words of Edith Nawakwi, "it was like somebody is pointing a gun to your head".[131]

The government did try to address these tax breaks in 2008 and as such increased taxes. In his 2008 budget speech the then Minister of Finance, Ng'andu Magande announced that there would be a new tax regime governing the mines in which copper revenues would "adequately contribute to the advancement and the social and economic welfare of the people of Zambia".[132] As such, the government purported to cancel all development agreements through the Mines and Minerals Development Act of 2008, which repealed and replaced the Mines and Minerals Act of 1995. In addition to this, the government then raised the corporate tax from 25% to 35%. The mineral royalty was raised from 0.6% to 3%.

127 See for example the Mopani Copper Mines Development Agreement, available at Minewatch Zambia http://www.minewatchzambia.com/agreements.html.

128 Evaristus Oshionebo, "Stabilization Clauses in Natural Resource Extraction Contracts: Legal, Economic and Social Implications for Developing Countries" (2010) 10 *Asper Review of International Business & Trade Law* 1, 18.

129 John Lungu, *The Politics of Reforming Zambia's Mining Tax Regime* (Southern Africa Resource Watch 2009) 16.

130 See the Ministerial Statement on the Status of Mining Taxation by the Hon. Situmbeko Musokotwane http://www.parliament.gov.zm/index.php?option=com_docman&task=doc_view&gid=770.

131 Edith Nawakwi quoted in Lungu (n 129) 16.

132 Budget Address by The Hon. Ng'andu P. Magande, MP Minister Of Finance And National Planning: Delivered To The National Assembly on 25th January 2008 http://www.parliament.gov.zm/index.php?option=com_docman&task=doc_view&gid=242.

A windfall tax was also introduced and this was triggered by pressure at various levels. It was hoped that these measures would bring in additional revenue of $415 million in 2008.[133]

The difficulty with these changes is that they rendered mining operations more onerous. The effective tax rates for high cost mines ranged between 64% and 96% and for low cost mines between 57% and 64%. This was clearly above the intended rate of 47%.[134] Because these changes rendered mining operations more onerous, mining companies resisted them. Furthermore, it was noted that the windfall tax had some major flaws and was weak in design. This was further compounded by the fact that world copper prices had fallen due to the effects of the global financial crisis.[135] The government thus proceeded to reverse these taxes in 2009. The Zambian tax regime has undergone many changes since.[136]

The cancellation of development agreements in 2008 became a source of liability for the government of Zambia.[137] This is evinced by the fact that First Quantum Minerals Limited initiated arbitral proceedings against the government of Zambia in the United Kingdom. First Quantum Mining Limited contended that the government of Zambia had arbitrarily breached the development agreement concerning Bwana Mkubwa. This was eventually withdrawn by First Quantum. Had the case gone forward, the government of Zambia may well have had to compensate the investor.

In a similar vein, the legislation pertaining to gender rights and equality in the Republic of Zambia, creates new obligations. With these new obligations come financial consequences for the mining companies. For example, under the Gender Equity and Equality Act, it has been seen that private corporations all have to draft codes on gender equality within their organizations. They are also under an obligation to make reports to the relevant authorities. In addition to this, they are also charged with actually enforcing the law through various measures. These include, for instance, undertaking regular audits and also creating a rewards system for compliance. The Employment Code Act also creates new obligations. For example, maternity leave can now go up to 18 weeks with full pay. All these aspects will have financial consequences on the investor. This, in turn, may be a source of liability to the host State, in that the investor could be on firm ground to initiate arbitral proceedings against the host State. If such a thing were to happen, the host State may be reluctant to develop any further laws, which, in turn, may hinder the fight for gender equity and equality in the Republic of Zambia.

133 Lungu (n 129) 19.

134 Ministerial Statement on the Status of Mining Taxation http://www.parliament.gov.zm/index.php?option=com_docman&task=doc_view&gid=770.

135 Savior Mwambwa, Aaron Griffiths and Andreas Kahler, *A Fool's Paradise? Zambia's Mining Tax Regime* (Centre for Trade Policy and Development 2010) 7.

136 See generally Ng'ambi (n 7).

137 "First Quantum Minerals Drops Lawsuit against Zambian Government Filed in the UK" (14th March 2014) *Lusaka Times* https://www.lusakatimes.com/2014/03/02/first-quantum-minerals-drops-lawsuit-zambian-government-filed-uk/.

5.6 Conclusion

It could thus be concluded that Zambia relies heavily on its mining industry. In the early part of the millennium, the process of attracting foreign direct investment into the Republic of Zambia, was fostered through development agreements, as authorized by the Mines and Minerals Act of 1995. Included within these development agreements were stabilization clauses. The general essence of these clauses were to ensure that the government does not pass any legislation that has a material adverse effect on the investment.

It has been seen from this chapter that since then, the government has passed various pieces of legislation. These have, quite rightly, had the effect of improving gender equity and equality in the republic of Zambia, on private entities. In principle, these Acts apply to investors as well. However, the difficulty that arises is the pecuniary consequences of applying these new gender laws. From the preceding chapter, it has been seen that in the event that development of human rights laws in general create more financial obligations on the investor, then the State would have to compensate the investor for this. Equally, it is advanced that in the event that these new pieces of legislation on gender create increased financial obligations on the State, then this might be a source of liability against the government of the Republic of Zambia. Now that this has been revealed, the question remains: will the prospect of a financial burden of this sort deter governments from further developing legislation on gender equity and equality in the Republic of Zambia?

6 Conclusion

6.1 Introductory remarks

Foreign direct investment involves the transfer of tangible or intangible assets from one jurisdiction to the other. The purpose of this transfer of tangible and intangible assets is to generate wealth. Typically, foreign direct investment is fostered through concession agreements. These concessions are typically drafted in such a way that the investor is allowed to explore and exploit natural resources, whilst remitting mineral royalties and other taxes to the host State.

To encourage the flow of investment, host States will also give a number of fiscal incentives. However, there are concerns as to whether these incentives will continue to subsist once the investment has been sunk and operations have commenced. For this reason, investors insist on the insertion of stabilization clauses. These effectively free the municipal law of the host State for the period of time stipulated within the contract. They thus immunize the concession agreement from any administrative or legislative measures that have a material adverse effect on the contractual rights within the concession. Breach of this undertaking invariably means that the host State is liable to compensate the investor.

The difficulty with this, as seen in this book, is that this raises human rights concerns. This is owing to the fact that developing new human rights legislation will mean an increase in the obligations of foreign investors, especially their operating costs. Therefore, the host State may be liable to compensate the investor in the event that new human rights legislation leads to an increase in operating costs. The pecuniary consequences of this, may mean that the host State is precluded or deterred from passing any new human rights laws including new legislation enhancing gender equity and equality within its jurisdiction. The aim of this chapter is to give an overview of this book and the themes covered, before rendering our final concluding remarks.

6.2 An overview of this book

6.2.1 Introductory chapter

The aim of the introductory chapter was to give a general overview of the international standards relating to investment protection. From this chapter it was seen that an international minimum standard on investment protection was not seen as necessary before 1945. This is owing to the fact that the regime pertaining to foreign direct investment existed within the context of the colonial legal framework. The legal systems of colonial powers and those of their colonies were inextricably linked. Thus, any investment protections needed within the colonies, were provided by the colonial power itself.

This position was considerably altered after the end of the Second World War. This period saw the dissolution of most of the world's empires and the emergence of independent States. These States asserted both their political and economic independence. Economic independence meant greater control over natural resources. Out of this, the principle of permanent sovereignty over natural resources was born.

6.2.2 The principle permanent sovereignty over natural resources

The principle of permanent sovereignty over natural resources espouses that host States can do whatsoever they wish with natural resources found within their jurisdiction. This principle was espoused under a number of General Assembly Resolutions. These included General Assembly Resolution 1803 and the Charter on the Economic Rights and Duties of States. These Resolutions stipulated that the host State had the right to permanent sovereignty over natural resources. Emanating from this right for example, was the right to nationalize and the right to regulate foreign investment.

There were concerns as to the legitimacy of this right, given the fact that it emanated mainly from General Assembly Resolutions and therefore was not binding. On the other hand, it was argued that the process of negotiating and adopting General Assembly Resolutions means they are evidence of consensus among States and therefore the principles espoused therein become evidence of customary international law. This view was endorsed in this book, because it is supported by international arbitral tribunals and the International Court of Justice.

A plethora of rights arise out of the doctrine of permanent sovereignty over natural resources. These include: (1) The right to freely dispose of natural resources, (2) the right to explore and exploit natural resources freely, (3) the right to use natural resources for national development and (4) the right to regulate foreign investment. In addition, the following duties emanate from the principle of permanent sovereignty over natural resources: (1) the duty to exercise permanent sovereignty over natural resources for the purposes of national development, (2) the duty to respect the rights of indigenous groups, (3) the duty to treat investors in accordance with international law and (4) the duty to compensate the investor in the event that the State unilaterally terminates a concession agreement.

Of particular importance here is the right to freely dispose of natural resources, as it is the basis upon which States enter into concession agreements with investors. The right to permanent sovereignty over natural resources is also frequently invoked, when States proceed to nationalize or impose regulatory measures that have a material adverse effect on the investor. As a result, investors will often insist on certain protections, including the insertion of stabilization clauses in the concession agreement.

6.2.3 Protections against political risk

Chapter 3 examines looked at political risk and the ways in which investors choose to protect themselves, especially through stabilization clauses. This chapter first starts by discussing the resource nationalism cycle. This describes a situation where the host State seeks to exert more control over their natural resource. This could either include nationalizing assets or raising taxes. To avert this, there is a plethora of contractual and extra-contractual protections available to investors.

Investors can, for example, protect themselves through investment insurance. Government backed investment insurance includes the Overseas Private Investment Corporation (OPIC), which provides insurance to American corporations investing overseas. There is also the Multilateral Investment Guarantee Agency (MIGA), which exists to protect investment in developing countries. There are also a number of investment insurance schemes run by private entities. Investors also have protection through multilateral treaties and Bilateral Investment Treaties. For example, investors are protected by "umbrella clauses" contained within Bilateral Investment Treaties. Moreover, there are a number of contractual clauses that investors may rely on. There are for example, arbitration clauses, which ensure that the dispute is heard by a neutral forum operating above the fray of the national judicial system of the host State. The parties can also insert choice-of-law clauses, indicating that the law of a nation other than the host State will govern the agreement. Finally, the parties may insert stabilization clauses which seek to immunize investors from any acts of the host State that will have a material adverse effect on the investor.

Stabilization clauses are a promise from the host State that they will not use their administrative or legislative prerogatives to override the terms of the concession agreement. These effectively freeze the law or at least ensure that no provision in the concession may be altered without the mutual agreement of the host State and the investor. As such, stabilization clauses act as a buffer against the advanced stages of the resource nationalism cycle. It has been seen from the case law that arbitral tribunals uphold such clauses. There may be contentions that stabilization clauses militate against the principle of permanent sovereignty over natural resources. However, such contentions are not looked upon with a very kindly eye by tribunals. Arbitral tribunals instead opine that entering into concession agreements with stabilization clauses is a facet of permanent sovereignty over natural resources. Such sovereignty is surrendered with respect to such contracts and therefore cannot be invoked as a reason to excuse themselves from their contractual obligations.

From this it is clear that breach of agreements containing stabilization clauses elicits payment of compensation to the investor. The prospect of paying such compensation, may deter host States from developing new human rights, which was the topic of discussion in Chapter 4.

6.2.4 Stabilization clauses and human rights

Chapter 4 discussed the impact of stabilization clauses on human rights. The aim of stabilization clauses is to immunize investors from the non-commercial risks associated with foreign direct investment. Compensation becomes payable in the event that the State unilaterally abrogates the concession agreement. When determining the amount of compensation payable, the State will take into account the legitimate expectations of the investor, during the timeframe that the concession was meant to subsist.

That the State is liable to compensate the investor once it breaches the concession agreement, is unquestionable. There are two standards of compensation under the international investment law regime. These are the Hull Principle and the appropriate compensation standard. These were discussed at length in Chapter 4. It was concluded in this chapter that regardless of the standard adopted, lost future profits (*lucrum cessans*) are typically considered in the compensation award.

The fact that the host State has to compensate the investor, may act as a deterrent for the development of new human rights. This is owing to the fact that new rights create new obligations on the investor. In this case, it may also mean an increase in operating costs of the investor. Such a scenario would elicit the payment of compensation from the host State to the investor. For developing countries, this has a chilling effect on their ability to develop the human rights regime in their countries. This also includes the ability to pass new legislation enhancing gender equity and equality within their jurisdictions.

6.2.5 Stabilization clauses and gender rights: a case study of Zambia

Chapter 5 discussed the effect of stabilization clauses on the Zambian government's ability to enhance gender equity and equality laws within Zambia. It was noted that the process of fostering foreign direct investment in the Zambian mining industry is processed through development agreements. Such agreements set out the rights and obligations of the State and the investor. They also contain tax incentives. To ensure that these incentives subsist for the duration of the contract, there are also stabilization clauses contained therein.

The difficulty that may arise is that the government of Zambia has passed various pieces of legislation since entering into these development agreements. These have enhanced gender equity and equality in Zambia. However, they may also have an impact on the obligations of foreign investors, which, in turn, also increases their operating costs. Such a scenario would be a source of liability for the host State. Investors may exercise the option to sue the host State, just as First Quantum Minerals Limited did over the cancellation of the Bwana Mkubwa Development Agreement.

Bibliography

"Transforming Our World: The 2030 Agenda for Sustainable Development" Resolution adopted by the General Assembly on 25 September 2015 A/RES/70/1, available at https://www.un.org/ga/search/view_doc.asp?symbol=A/RES/70/1&Lang=E

Abi-Saab, G., "Progressive Development of the Principles and Norms of International Law Relating to the New International Economic Order" in UN Doc. A/39/504/ Add. 1, 23rd October 1973

Akinsanya, A., "Permanent Sovereignty over Natural Resources and the Future of Foreign Investment" (1978) 7 *Journal of International Studies* 124

Al Faruque, A., "Renegotiation and Adaptation of Petroleum Contracts: The Quest for Equilibrium and Stability" (2008) 9 *Journal of World Investment and Trade* 113

Amnesty International, *Human Rights on the Line: The Baku-Tbilisi-Ceyhan Pipeline Project*, (Amnesty International UK 2003)

Amnesty International, *Contracting Out of Human Rights – The Chad Pipeline Project* (Amnesty International UK 2005)

Arbtali, E., "Political Regimes, Investment Risk and Resource Nationalism: An Empirical Analysis" 21, http://regconf.hse.ru/uploads/7da62134fab330f54f067e5cd2e603c40298cd7e.pdf

Asante, S.K.B., "Restructuring Transnational Mineral Agreements" (1979) 73 *American Journal of International Law* 335

Baker, J.C., *Foreign Direct Investment in Less Developed Countries: The Role of ICSID and MIGA* (Quorum Books 1999)

Banerjee, S.K., "The Concept of Permanent Sovereignty over Natural Resources: An Analysis" (1968) 8 *Indian Journal of International Law* 515

Barrera-Hernándes, L., "Sovereignty over Natural Resources under Examination: The Inter-American System for Human Rights and Natural Resource Allocation" (2006) 12 *Annual Survey of International and Comparative Law* 43

Baxter, R.R., "International Law in 'Her Infinite Variety'" (1980) 29 *International and Comparative Law Quarterly* 549

Bermann, G.A., "The 'Gateway' Problem in International Commercial Arbitration" (2012) 37 *Yale Journal of International Law* 1, 14–15

Bernardini, P., "Stabilization and Adaptation in Oil and Gas Investments" (2008) 1 *Journal of World Energy Law and Business* 98

Bleicher, S.A., "The Legal Significance of Re-Citation of General Assembly Resolutions" (1969) 63 *American Journal of International Law* 444

Borehand, E.M., "Contractual Claims in International Law" (1913) 13 *Columbia Law Review* 457

Bowett, D.W., "State Contracts with Aliens: Contemporary Developments on Compensation for Termination or Breach" (1988) 49 *British Yearbook of International Law* 49

Boyle, A. and Chinkin, C.K, *The Making of International Law* (OUP 2007)

Brölmann, C., Lefeber, R. and Zieck, M. (eds), *Peoples and Minorities in International Law* (Kluwer 1993)

Brooker, P., *Non-Democratic Regimes: Theory, Government and Politics* (Macmillan 2000)

Brown, C. (ed), *Commentaries on Selected Model Investment Treaties* (OUP 2013)

Brownlie, I., *Principles of Public International Law* (7th edn, OUP 2008)

Burdette, M., "Nationalization in Zambia: A Critique of Bargaining Theory" (1977) 11 *Canadian Journal of African Studies* 471

Carbonneau, T.E. (ed), *Lex Mercatoria and Arbitration* (Kluwer 1998)

Cernic, L.J., "Corporate Human Rights Obligations under Stabilization Clauses" (2010) 11 *German Law Journal* 210

Chatterjee, S.K., "The Stabilization Clause Myth in Investment Agreements" (1988) 5 *Journal of International Arbitration* 97

Chowdhury, S.R., "Permanent Sovereignty over Natural Resources: Substratum of the Seoul Declaration" in de Wart, P., Peters, P. and Denters, E. (eds), *International Law and Development* (Martinus Nijhoff 1988) 61

Chua, A., "The Privatization-Nationalization Cycle: The Link between Markets and Ethnicity in Developing Countries" (1995) 95 *Columbia Law Review* 95

Coale, T.B.M., "Stabilisation Clauses in International Petroleum Transactions" (2002) 30 *Denver Journal of International Law and Policy* 217

Cook, A., "Kompetenz-Kompetenz: Varying Approaches and a Proposal for a Limited Form of Kompetenz-Kompetenz" (2014) 42 *Pepperdine Law Review* 17

Cotula, L., "Reconciling Regulatory Stability and Evolution of Environmental Standards in Investment Contracts: Towards a Rethink of Stabilization Clauses" (2008) 1 *Journal of World Energy and Business* 158.

Country Gender Profile: Zambia Final Report March 2016 Japan International Cooperation Agency (JICA) Japan Development Service Co., Ltd. (JDS)

Crane, A., Palazzo, G., and Spence, L.J., "Contesting the Value of 'Creating Shared Value'" (2014) 56 *California Management Review* 130

Crawford, J., *The International Law Commission's Articles on State Responsibility, Introduction, Text and Commentaries* (Cambridge University Press 2002)

Crawford, J., *The Creation of States in International Law* (2nd edn, OUP 2006)

Curtis, C.T., "The Legal Security of Economic Development Agreements" (1988) 29 *Harvard International Law Journal* 317

Dawson, F.G. and Weston, B.H., "'Prompt, Adequate and Effective': A Universal Standard of Compensation" (1962) 30 *Fordham Law Review* 727

de Aréchaga, E.J., "State Responsibility for the Nationalization of Foreign Owned Property" (1978) 11 *New York University Journal of Law and Politics* 179

de Sá Ribeiro, M.R. "Sovereignty over Natural Resources Investment Law and Expropriation: The Case of Bolivia and Brazil" (2009) 2 *Journal of World Energy Law & Business* 129

de Schutter O. (ed), *Transnational Corporations and Human Rights* (Bloomsbury Publishing 2006)

de Vries, H., "The Enforcement of Economic Development Agreements with Foreign States" (1984) 62 *University of Detroit Law Review* 1

de Wart, P. and Denters, E., *International Law and Development* (Matinus Nijhoff 1988)

Diamond, L., *Developing Democracy: Toward Consolidation* (Johns Hopkins 1999)

Dolzer, R. and Schreuer, C., *Principles of International Investment Law* (2nd edn, OUP 2012)

Dolzer, R. and Stevens, M., *Bilateral Investment Treaties* (Martinus Nijhoff 1995)

Dolzer, R., "New Foundations of the Law of Expropriation of Alien Property" (1981) 75 *American Journal of International Law* 553

Dolzer, R., "Expropriation for Nationalization" (1985) 8 *Encyclopedia of Public International Law* 214

Drahozal, C.R., "Contracting Out of National Law: An Empirical Look at the New Law Merchant" (2005) 80 *Notre Dame Law Review* 523

Dufrense, R., "The Opacity of Oil: Oil Corporations, Internal Violence, and International Law" (2004) 36 *New York University Journal of International Law and Politics* 331

Duriugbo, E., "Permanent Sovereignty and Peoples' Ownership of Natural Resources in International Law" (2006) 38 *George Washington International Law Review* 33

Eisenberg, A., "Different Constitutional Formulations of Compensation Clauses" (1993) 9 *South African Journal of Human Rights* 412

Elias, T.O., *The Modern Law of Treaties* (Oceania 1974)

Emeka, J.N., "Anchoring Stabilization Clauses in International Petroleum Contracts" (2008) 42 *International Lawyer* 1317, 1319

Faruque, A., "Validity and Efficacy of Stabilization Clauses: Legal Protection vs. Functional Value" (2006) 23 *Journal of International Arbitration* 317

Fatouros, A.A., "International Law and the Internationalized Contract" (1980) 74 *American Journal of International Law* 134–141

Final Documents of the Tenth Conference of Heads of State or Government of Non-Aligned Countries, Jakarta, 1–6 September 1992

Friedland, P.D. and Wong, E., "Measuring Damages for the Deprivation of Income-Producing Assets: ICSID Case Studies" (1991) 6 *ICSID Review Foreign Investment Law Journal* 400

Gann, P.B., "Compensation Standard for Expropriation" (1984) 23 *Columbia Journal of Transnational Law* 615

Garcia-Amador, F.V., *Special Rapporteur's Report* (International Law Commission 1959)

Gess, K.S., "Permanent Sovereignty over Natural Resources: An Analytical Review of the United Nations Declaration and Its Genesis" (1964) 13 *International and Comparative Law Quarterly* 398

Goodman, R.E.M. and Parkhomenko, Y., "Does the Chorzów Factory Standard Apply in Investment Arbitration? A Contextual Reappraisal" (2017) 32 *ICSID Review* 304

Gotanda, J.Y., "Renegotiation and Adaptation Clauses in International Contracts Revisited" (2003) 36 *Vanderbilt Journal of Transnational Law* 1461

Guriev, S., Kolotilin, A., and Sonin, K., "Determinants of Nationalization in the Oil Sector: A Theory and Evidence from Panel Data" (2009) 27 *The Journal of Law, Economics, & Organization* 301.

Guzman, A., "Why LDCs Sign Treaties That Hurt Them: Explaining the Popularity of Bilateral Investment Treaties" (1998) 38 *Virginia Journal of International Law* 639

Hackworth, G., *Digest of International Law: Volume 3* (US Government Printing Office 1942)

Halabi, S.F., "Efficient Contracting Between Foreign Investors and Host States: Evidence from Stabilization Clauses" (2011) 31 *Northwestern Journal of International Law and Business* 261

Hossain, K. and Chowdhury, S.R. (eds), *Permanent Sovereignty over Natural Resources* (Frances Printer 1984)

Hossain, K. (ed), *Legal Aspects of the New International Economic Order* (Frances Pinter 1980)

Hyde, J.N., "Permanent Sovereignty over Natural Wealth and Resources" (1956) 50 *American Society of International Law* 854

Ingolfsson, S.H., *Stabilization Clauses in Investment Agreements – A Human Rights and Development Perspective* (Graduate Thesis Master of Laws Programme, Lund 2012)

Inniss, A.B., "Rethinking Political Risk Insurance: Incentives for Investor Risk Mitigation" (2010) 16 *Southwestern Journal of International Law* 477

Jensen, N.M., *Nation-States and the Multinational Corporation* (Princeton 2006)

Jensen, N.M., "Political Risk, Democratic Institutions and Foreign Direct Investment" (2008) 70 *The Journal of Politics* 1040

Keohane, R.O. and Milner, H.V (eds), *Internationalization and Domestic Politics* (Cambridge University Press 1996)

Kerwin, G.J., "The Role of United Nations General Assembly Resolutions in Determining Principles of International Law in United States Courts" (1983) 4 *Duke Law Journal* 876

Koskemeni, M., "What Use for Sovereignty Today" (2011) 1 *Asian Journal of International Law* 61–70

Li, Q., "Democracy, Autocracy and Expropriation of Foreign Direct Investment" (2009) 42 *Comparative Political Studies* 1098

Lieblich, W.C., "Determinations by International Tribunals of the Economic Value of Expropriated Enterprises" (1990) 7 *Journal of International Arbitration* 37

Lowenfeld, A., "Investment Agreements and International Law" (2003) 42 *Columbia Journal of Transnational Law* 123

Lowenfeld, A., *International Economic Law* (2nd edn, OUP 2008)

Lungu, J., "Copper Mining Agreements in Zambia: Renegotiation or Law Reform?" (2008) 117 *Review of African Political Economy* 403

Lungu, J., *The Politics of Reforming Zambia's Mining Tax Regime* (Southern Africa Resource Watch 2009)

Maniruzzaman, A.F.M., "International Development Law as Applicable Law to Economic Development Agreements: A Prognostic View" (2001) 20 *Wisconsin International Law Journal* 1

Maniruzzaman, A.F.M., "Some Reflections on Stabilisation Techniques in International Petroleum, Gas and Mineral Agreements" (2005) 4 *International Energy Law and Taxation Review* 96

Maniruzzaman, A.F.M., "The Issue of Resource Nationalism: Risk Engineering and Dispute Management in the Oil and Gas Industry" (2009) 5 *Journal of Oil and Gas Law* 79

Marboe, I., "Compensation and Damages in International Law: The Limits of 'Fair Market Value'" (2006) 7 *Journal of World Investment and Trade* 723

Marsh, B., "Preventing the Inevitable: The Benefits of Contractual Risk Engineering in the Light of Venezuela's Recent Oil Field Nationalization" (2008) 13 *Stanford Journal of Law Business & Finance* 453

Martin, A., *Mining their Own Business: Zambia's Struggle against Western Control* (Hutchinson 1972)

McCrudden, C., *Anti-Discrimination Law* (Dartmouth 1991)

McLachlan, C., Shore L., and Weiniger, M., *International Investment Arbitration: Substantive Principles* (OUP 2010)

Mendelson, M.H., "Compensation for Expropriation: The Case Law" (1985) 79 *American Journal of International Law* 414

Miranda, L.A., "The Role of International Law in Intrastate Natural Resource Allocation: Sovereignty, Human Rights, and People-Based Development" (2012) 45 *Vanderbilt Journal of Transnational Law* 785

Montembault, B., "The Stabilisation of State Contracts Using the Example of Oil Contracts: A Return of the Gods of Olympia" (2003) 6 *International Business Law Journal* 593

Muchlinski, P., *Multinational Enterprises and the Law* (2nd edn, OUP 2007)

Muchlinski, P., Ortino F., and Schreuer, C. (eds), *The Oxford Handbook of International Investment Law* (OUP 2008)

Mwaanga, P., Silondwa, M., Kasali, G., and Banda, P.M., "Preliminary Review of Mine Air Pollution in Zambia" (2019) 5 Heliyon https://www.sciencedirect.com/science/article/pii/S2405844019361456

Mwambwa, S., Griffiths, A., and Kahler, A., *A Fool's Paradise? Zambia's Mining Tax Regime* (Centre for Trade Policy and Development 2010)

Mwenda, K.K. "Legal Aspects of Foreign Direct Investment in Zambia" (1999) 6 *Murdoch University Electronic Journal of Law* 35

Nakagawa, J., *Nationalization, Natural Resources and International Investment Law: Contractual Relationship as a Dynamic Bargaining Process* (Routledge 2018)

Nazneen, S., Hickey, S, and Sifaki (eds), *Negotiating Gender Equity in the Global South: The Politics of Domestic Violence Policy* (Routledge 2019)

Ndulo, M. "Mining Legislation and Mineral Development in Zambia" (1986) 19 *Cornell International Law Journal* 1

Ndulo, N., "The Nationalization of the Zambian Copper Industry" (1974) 6 *Zambia Law Journal* 55

Ng'ambi, S.P., "Stabilisation Clauses and the Zambian Windfall Tax" (2010) 1 *Zambia Social Science Journal* 107

Ng'ambi, S.P., "Mineral Taxation and Resource Nationalism in Zambia" (2015) 2 *Southern African Journal of Policy and Development* 6

Ng'ambi, S.P., "Permanent Sovereignty over Natural Resources and the Sanctity of Contracts, from the Angle of Lucrum Cessans" (2015) 12 *Loyola University Chicago International Law Review* 153

Ng'ambi, S.P., *Resource Nationalism in International Investment Law* (Routledge 2016)

Ng'ambi, S.P., *Understanding Investment Law in Zambia* (Juta 2016)

Nussbaum, A., "The Arbitration between the Lena Goldfields, Ltd. and the Soviet Government" (1950–51) 36 *Cornell Law Quarterly* 31

Nwaokoro, J., "Enforcing Stabilization of International Energy Contracts" (2013) 3 *Journal of World Energy Law & Business* 103

Oshionebo, E., "Stabilization Clauses in Natural Resource Extraction Contracts: Legal, Economic and Social Implications for Developing Countries" (2010) 10 *Asper Review of International Business & Trade Law* 1

Overseas Private Investment Corporation, *OPIC Handbook* (OPIC 2006) http://www.opic.gov/sites/default/files/docs/OPIC_Handbook.pdf

Paasirvirta, E., "Internationalization and Stabilization of Contracts Versus State Sovereignty' (1989) 60 *British Yearbook of International Law* 315

Paasivirta, E., *Participation of States in International Contracts and Arbitral Settlement of Disputes* (Lakimiesluton Kustannus 1990)

Penrose, E., Joffé, G., and Stevens, P., "Nationalisation of Foreign-Owned Property for a Public Purpose: An Economic Perspective on Appropriate Compensation" (1992) 55 *Modern Law Review* 351

Pereira, R. and Gough, O., "Permanent Sovereignty over Natural Resources in the 21st Century: Natural Resource Governance and the Right to Self-Determination of Indigenous Peoples under International Law" (2013) 14 *Melbourne Journal of International Law* 1

Petrov, N., Lipman M., and Hale, H.H., *Overmanaged Democracy in Russia: Governance Implications of Hybrid Regimes* (Carnegie Endowment for International Peace 2010)

Porter, M. and Kramer, M., "Creating Shared Value: How to Reinvent Capitalism and Unleash a Wave of Innovation and Growth" (2011) 89 *Harvard Business Review* 1

Qureshi, A. and Ziegler, A., *International Economic Law* (3rd edn, Sweet & Maxwell 2011)

Rosen, A.J., "Arbitration under Private International Law: The Doctrines of Separability and Compétence de la Compétence" (1993) 17 *Fordham International Law Journal* 599

Rousseau, C.E., *Mélangues offerts à Charles Rousseau* (A Pedone 1974)

Rubin, A.P., *Recueil des Cours* (Sijthoff and Noordhoff 1979)

Sands, P. and Klein, P., *Bowett's Law of International Institutions* (6th edn, Sweet & Maxwell 2009)

Sardanis, A., *A Venture in Africa: The Challenges of African Business* (I.B. Tauris 2007)

Sardanis, A., *Africa: Another Side of the Coin: Northern Rhodesia's Final Years and Zambia's Nationhood* (I.B. Tauris 2011)

Schachter, O., "Compensation for Expropriation" (1984) 78 *American Journal of International Law* 121–130

Schemberg, A., *Stabilization Clauses and Human Rights: A Research Project Conducted for IFC and United Nations Special Representative to the Secretary General on Business and Human Rights.* March 11 2008

Schmitter, P.C. and Karl, T.L., "What Democracy Is . . . and Is Not" (1991) 2 *Journal of Democracy* 75

Schreuer, C.H., "Unjustified Enrichment in International Law" (1974) 22 *American Journal of Comparative Law* 281–301

Schrijver, N., *Sovereignty over Natural Resources: Balancing Rights and Duties* (CUP 1997)

Schrijver, N., "Natural Resource Management and Sustainable Development" in Weiss, T.G. and Daws, S. (eds), *The Oxford Handbook on the United Nations* (OUP 2007) 596

Schrijver, N., "Natural Resources, Permanent Sovereignty over" (2010) *Max Planck Encyclopedia of Public International Law* 8

Schwebel, S.M., "The Story of the U.N.'s Declaration on Permanent Sovereignty over Natural Resources" (1963) 49 *American Bar Association Journal* 463

Seatzu T.T.F. and Trevisanut S. (eds), *Foreign Investment and Common Concerns: An International Law Perspective* (Routledge 2013)

Shan, W., "Is Calvo Dead?" (2007) 55 *American Journal of Comparative Law* 123

Shihata, I.F.I. "The Multilateral Investment Guarantee Agency" (1986) 20 *International Lawyer* 485

Sikamo, J., Mwanza, A., and Mweemba, C., "Copper Mining in Zambia – History and Future" (2016) 116 *Journal of the Southern African Institute of Mining and Metallurgy* 491

Smith, R.J., "The United States Government Perspective on Expropriation and Investment in Developing Countries" (1976) 9 *Vanderbilt Journal of Transnational Law* 517

Sohn L.B. and Baxter, R.R., "Responsibility of States for Injuries to the Economic Interests of Aliens" (1961) 55 *American Journal of International Law* 545

Sornarajah, M., "Compensation for Expropriation. The Emergence of New Standards" (1979) 13 *Journal of World Trade Law* 108

Sornarajah, M., *The International Law on Foreign Investment* (3rd edn, CUP 2010)

Sornarajah, M., *The Settlement of Foreign Investment Disputes* (Kluwer 2000)

Subedi, S., *International Investment Law: Reconciling Policy and Principle* (2nd edn, Hart Publishing 2012)

Suratgar, D., "Considerations Affecting Choice of Law Clauses in Contracts between Governments and Foreign Nationals" (1962) 2 *Indian Journal of International Law* 273

Taverne, B., *Petroleum, Industry and Governments: A Global Study of the Involvement of Industry and Government in the Production and Use of Petroleum* (2nd edn, Kluwer 2008)

Thornberry, P., "Self Determination, Minorities, Human Rights: A Review of International Instruments" (1989) 38 *International and Comparative Law Quarterly* 867

Thornberry, P., *International Law and the Rights of Minorities* (OUP 1991)

Vandevelde, K.J., "A Brief History of International Investment Agreements" (2005) 12 *University of California Davis Journal of International Law and Policy* 157, 158

Várady, T., Barceló, J.J., and Von Mehren, A.T., *International Commercial Arbitration: A Transnational Perspective* (3rd edn, Thomson 2006)

Vedeer, V.V., "The Lena Goldfields Arbitration: The Historical Roots of the Three Ideas" (1998) 47 *International and Comparative Law Quarterly* 747

Vernon, R., *Sovereignty at Bay: The Multinational Spread of US Enterprises* (Longman 1971)

Von Mehren, R.B. and Kourides, N.P., "International Arbitration between States and Foreign Private Parties: The Libyan Nationalization Cases" (1981) 75 *American Journal of International Law* 476

von Soest, C. "How Does Neopatrimonialism Affect the African State's Revenues? The Case of Tax Collection in Zambia" (2007) 45 *Journal of Modern African Studies* 621, 636

Wälde, T.W. and Ndi, G. "Stabilizing International Investment Commitments: International Law Versus Contract Interpretation" (1996) 31 *Texas International Law Journal* 215

Wälde, T.W., "Renegotiating Acquired Rights in the Oil and Gas Industries: Industry and Political Cycles Meet the Rule of Law" (2008) 1 *Journal of World Energy Law and Business* 55

Warden-Fernandez, J., "The Permanent Sovereignty over Natural Resources: How It Has Been Accommodated Within the Evolving Economy" (2000) 4 *CEPMLP Annual Review* 3

Weiss, T.G. and Daws, S. (eds), *The Oxford Handbook on the United Nations* (OUP 2007)

Wong, J., "Umbrella Clauses in Bilateral Investment Treaties: Of Breaches of Contract, Treaty Violations, and the Divide between Developing and Developed Countries in Foreign Investment Disputes" (2006) 14 *George Mason Law Review* 137

Woodhouse, E.J., "The Obsolescing Bargain Redux? Foreign Investment in the Electric Power Sector in Developing Countries" (2006) 38 *New York University Journal of International Law and Politics* 121

World Bank, "World Bank Guidelines, on the Treatment of Foreign Direct Investment" (1992) 31 *International Legal Materials* 1379

World Bank, *World Development Report of 1979*

Yackee, J.W., "*Pacta Sunt Servanda* and State Promises to Foreign Investors before Bilateral Investment Treaties: Myth and Reality" (2009) 32 *Fordham International Law Journal* 1550

Yelpaala, K., "In Search of Effective Policies for Foreign Direct Investment: Alternatives to Tax Incentive Policies" (1985) 7 *Northwestern Journal of International Law and Business* 208

Ziegler, A.R. and Gratton, L., "Investment Insurance" in Muchlinski, P., Ortino, F. and Schreuer, C. (eds), *The Oxford Handbook of International Investment Law* (OUP 2008) 526

Zongwe, D.P., "The Contribution of Campbell v Zimbabwe to the Foreign Investment Law on Expropriations" (2010) 2 *Namibia Law Journal* 31

Index

Note: Page numbers followed by "n" denote endnotes.

Access Bank 109n58
African Charter on Human and Peoples' Rights 96; Article 21(1) 24, 35
African Convention on the Conservation of Nature and Natural Resources (1968) 35
2030 Agenda for Sustainable Development (Agenda 2030) 100
Agip v Congo 26
AGIP v. Popular Republic of Congo 73–4, 89
AIG, *see* American Insurance Group (AIG)
Amazon Declaration (1989) 35; rights of indigenous peoples in 39, 39n115
AMCO Asia Corporation v Indonesia 27
American Insurance Group (AIG) 9, 51
Aminoil v Kuwait 17, 29, 30, 74–6, 88
Amnesty International 94, 96, 97
Anglo-American Corporation 120
applicable law clause 59
appropriate compensation 20, 34, 83–5, 128
Aramco v Saudi Arabia 30
arbitral award 58
arbitral tribunal 9, 10, 12–13, 29, 53, 56–8, 67, 72–5, 77, 81, 85, 88–90, 127
arbitration: advantages of 9–11; clauses 9, 50, 58–9; definition of 9
Argentina–United States BIT 119
Article I of First Protocol of the European Convention on Human Rights 84
Article II(2)(c) of United States-Romania BIT 54
Article II(3) of Convention on the Recognition and Enforcement of Foreign Arbitral Awards 9
Article IV of Treaty for Amazonian Co-operation (1978) 28
Article 1 of CERDS 31
Article 1(1) of Indigenous and Tribal People's Convention 36–7
Article 1(2) of International Covenant on Civil and Political Rights 24
Article 1(2) of International Covenant on Economic Social and Cultural Rights 35n101
Article 2(1) of CERDS 20
Article 2(2) of British Model Treaty 53
Article 2(2)(a) of CERDS 32
Article 2(4) of Italy-Jordan BIT 56
Article 3(a) of United Nations Convention to Combat Desertification 39–40
Article 3.5 of Netherlands-Poland BIT 54
Article 4(1) of Chinese Model Bilateral Investment Treaty (2003) 52
Article 5(d) of United Nations Convention to Combat Desertification 40
Article 6 of Geneva Convention Concerning Upper Silesia 42, 86
Article 7 of CERDS 29n79
Article 7 of Geneva Convention Concerning Upper Silesia 86
Article 8(2) of Declaration on the Rights of Indigenous Peoples 37
Article 10 of Declaration on the Rights of Indigenous Peoples 37–8
Article 10(3) of Draft Convention on State Responsibility (1961) 32
Article 11 of MIGA Convention 6, 51
Article 11 of Switzerland–Paraguay BIT 55
Article 12 of MIGA Convention 51
Article 12(1) of ILO Convention 38

Article 13 of Energy Charter Treaty 52n45
Article 13 of ILO Convention 39
Article 14 of MIGA Convention 51
Article 15 of ILO Convention 39
Article 15(1) of Biodiversity Convention (1992) 24n57
Article 16 of ILO Convention 39n114
Article 16 of Zambian Constitution 110
Article 16(1) of UNCITRAL Model Law on International Commercial Arbitration 10
Article 18(1) of Energy Charter Treaty (1994) 25
Article 18(2) of Energy Charter Treaty (1994) 25n58
Article 18(3) of Energy Charter Treaty (1994) 25
Article 19(1)(a) of United Nations Convention to Combat Desertification 40
Article 21(1) of African Charter on Human and Peoples' Rights 24, 35
Article 21.3 of TOTCO-Chad agreement 95
Article 24 of Declaration on the Rights of Indigenous Peoples 38
Article 25 of Declaration on the Rights of Indigenous Peoples 38
Article 25 of International Covenant on Economic Social and Cultural Rights 28
Article 27 in United Nations Covenant on Civil and Political Rights 37
Article 29 of Declaration on the Rights of Indigenous Peoples 38
Article 41(1) of ICSID Convention 10
Article 42(3) of ICSID Convention 89
Article 47 of International Covenant on Civil and Political Rights 28n73
Article 54(1) of ICSID Convention 10
Article 56(1)(a) of Convention on the Law of the Sea 28
Article 62 of Vienna Convention on the Law of Treaties 26–7
Article 193 of Convention on the Law of the Sea 30
Article 220(f) of Lomé IV Convention (1989) 29
Article 1110 of North American Free Trade Agreement 52
Asian Agricultural Ltd v Republic of Sri Lanka 82
authoritarian system 48

Banco Nacional de Cuba v Chase Manhattan Bank 84–5
Beijing Platform 105, 106, 113
Benevuti et Bonfant v People's Republic of Congo 89–90
Bilateral Investment Treaties (BITs) 2, 6, 11, 50–7, 119, 127; *see also* specific BITs
Bill of Rights 103, 110
Biodiversity Convention (1992) 24; Article 15(1) of 24n57
book value approach 81–2
BP v Libya 70
breach: of concession agreement 91, 94, 127; of contracts 15, 54, 56, 57, 70; of treaty 42; of umbrella clause 52–4
BTC pipeline project 96–8

Calvo, Carlos 3
Calvo Doctrine 3
Case Concerning German Interests in Upper Silesia 33–4, 86
case law on stabilization clauses 64–76; *Lena Goldfields, Ltd. v. U.S.S.R* 64–5; Libyan nationalization cases 68–72; *Sapphire International Petroleum Ltd. v. National Iranian Oil Co. (NIOC)* 65–6; *Saudi Arabia v. Arabian American Oil Co. (Aramco)* 67
CERDS, *see* Charter of Economic Rights and Duties of States (CERDS)
Certain German Interests in the Polish Upper Silesia 41
Chad-Cameroon Pipeline Project 94–6
change of circumstances 26–7, 27n69
Charter of Economic Rights and Duties of States (CERDS) 5, 18, 83–4, 126; Article 1 31; Article 2(1) 20; Article 2(2)(a) 32; Article 7 of 29n79; right to nationalize 34
Chinese Model Bilateral Investment Treaty (2003): Article 4(1) 52
choice of law clause 8, 50, 59, 69, 71, 127
Chubb and Zurich Emerging Markets Solution 51
CME v Czech Republic 81
CMS Gas v Argentina 57
Cobo, Martínez 36
Commission on Permanent Sovereignty 19
compensation 98, 128; adequacy of 43, 78; aim of 86; appropriate 83–5; book value approach 81–2; comprehensive balance sheet 82; going concern approach 80–1; indirect valuation

methods 80–2; principle of permanent sovereignty and 42–3; prompt, adequate and effective payment 80; purpose of 43; replacement cost approach 81; standards 79–85
Concession Agreement (1933) 61
concession agreements 1, 25, 45, 125; arbitration clause in 9–10; breach of 91, 94, 127; provisions 68–9; stabilization clauses in 120–3; standard 47, 68; termination of 7, 44, 59
Congo v Uganda 5, 23
Constitution of Zambia 103, 107, 118n112; Article 16 110; Bill of Rights 103, 110
contractual clauses 50, 58–60, 127
Convention Bological Diversity 39
Convention on the Elimination of all forms of Discrimination Against Women (CEDAW) 103, 105, 108
Convention on the Law of the Sea: Article 56(1)(a) 28; Article 193 30
Convention on the Recognition and Enforcement of Foreign Arbitral Awards 58
COTCO-Cameroon agreement (1997) 95
creeping expropriation 33
"cross-border subterranean resources" 64
customary international law 21–3, 27n29

DCF method, *see* discounted cash flow (DCF) method
Decision on Jurisdiction Enron Corporation and Ponderosa Assets, L.P v The Argentine Republic 119
Declaration on Gender and Development ("the Declaration") 105, 106
Declaration on the Rights of Indigenous Peoples: Article 8(2) 37; Article 10 37–8; Article 24 38; Article 25 38; Article 29 38
Delagoa case 90
development agreements 100, 121, 123
discounted cash flow (DCF) method 87
discrimination 42, 107
dispute settlement clause 58–9
doctrine of permanent sovereignty over natural resources, *see* principle of permanent sovereignty over natural resources
duties under principle of permanent sovereignty over natural resources 14, 126; compensations 42–3; national development 35–6; rights and interests of indigenous groups 36–40; treating investors in accordance with international law 40–2

East Timor Case 23
economic stabilization clause 62–3
ECT, *see* Energy Charter Treaty (ECT)
El Paso Energy International Company v Argentina 56
Employment Code Act, No. 3 (2019) 12, 100, 101, 104, 123; Minimum Employee Benefits 116, 118; Section 41 116–17, 116n95; Section 42 117; Section 43 117; Section 44 117; section 45 117; Section 46 117–18; Section 127 118
Energy Charter Treaty (ECT) 9; Article 18(1) 25; Article 18(2) 25n58; Article 18(3) 25
Eureko v Poland 54
European Court of Human Rights 31, 41, 42, 84

First Quantum Mining Limited 123
fiscal incentives 125
Fisheries Jurisdiction Case 28
foreign (direct) investment 1, 47, 125; benefits 7; in modern international law context 6–7
France-Hong Kong BIT (1995) 53

Gaddafi, Muammar 69
gender and investment, in Zambia 100–2; investor-State co-operation 102; legal framework 103–6; predictability of policy 102; sustainability of investments 101; themes and obligations in 106–20
Gender Equity and Equality Act (GEEA) No. 22 (2015) 12, 100, 101, 103, 107, 113, 123; Commission (*see* Gender Equity and Equality Commission); investor obligations 115–18; provisions 114; Section 15 107; Section 18(1) 115; Section 18(2) 115; Section 19(1) 115; Section 19(1)(e) 115; Section 23 108; Section 27(1) 116; Section 31 116
Gender Equity and Equality Commission 114
gender policy, in Zambia 101–2
General Assembly Resolution (1803) 4–5, 4n14
Georgia–Azerbaijan–Turkey IGA 97

Germany–Pakistan BIT (1959) 53
Global Witness 93
going concern approach 80–1
Guidelines on the Treatment of Foreign Direct Investment, World Bank 6

harmful work 117
Host Government Agreements (HGA) 97
host State-foreign investor relationship: agreements (*see* concession agreements); asymmetrical relationship 46; benefits 7
Hull, Cordell 3
Hull Principle 3, 8, 43, 80–2, 91, 128
human rights obligations, stabilization clauses and 15, 91, 128; BTC pipeline project 96–8; Chad-Cameroon Pipeline Project 94–6; Liberia-Mittal Steel Holdings AG, MDA 92–4

ICSID, *see* International Centre for Settlement of Investment Disputes (ICSID)
Indigenous and Tribal People's Convention, Article 1(1) 36–7
indigenous groups, rights and interests of 36–40
insurances: investment 9, 127; political risk 50, 51
intangibility clause 62
Intergovernmental Agreement (IGA) 97
International Centre for Settlement of Investment Disputes (ICSID) 89, 119; Article 41(1) of 10; Article 54(1) of 10
international compensation standards 79–80; appropriate compensation 83–5; Hull Principle 80–2
International Court of Justice: in *Fisheries Jurisdiction Case* 28; principle of permanent sovereignty over natural resources 23
International Covenant on Civil and Political Rights: Article 1(2) 24; Article 47 28n73
International Covenant on Economic Social and Cultural Rights: Article 1(2) 35n101; Article 25 28
international investment law: clash of ideologies 3; compensation standards under 79–91; evolution of 2–5; gender and human rights issues 11–13; mitigating political risk in 46–60
International Labour Organization (ILO): Convention concerning Indigenous and Tribal Peoples in Independent Countries 39, 39n114; Convention concerning the Protection and Integration of Indigenous and Other Tribal and Semi-Tribal Populations in Independent Countries (1957) 38
International Legal Assistance Consortium 93
International Tropical Timber Agreement (1994), Article 1(j) 40n117
investment arbitration 9–11
investment insurance 9, 127
investment protection 125–6; Calvo Doctrine 3; insurances 9; international standards for 1, 2; need for 2; non-commercial risks and 6, 7
investor–State disputes 118–20
Iranian Canada Oil Company (ICRAN) 65
Italy–Jordan BIT, Article 2(4) 56

James v United Kingdom 41
Joy Mining Machinery Limited v The Arabic Republic of Egypt 56

kompetenz-kompetenz principle 10

Lands Acquisition Act 103, 110; Section 11 120
Lena Goldfields, Ltd. v. U.S.S.R 3, 64–5, 87
Liberia–Mittal Steel Holdings AG, MDA 92–4
Libyan American Oil Company (LIAMCO) v Libya 5, 10, 22, 41, 59, 72, 87–8
Libyan nationalization cases 68–72; awards after 73–6; *BP v Libya* 70; *LIAMCO v Libya* 72; *Texaco Overseas Oil Petroleum Co./California Asiatic Oil Co. v Libya* 71–2
Libyan Petroleum Law (1955) 68
Lithgow v United Kingdom 31, 84
Lloyds of London 9, 51
Lomé IV Convention (1989): Article 220(f) 29
lost future profits 85–91

Magande, Ng'andu 122
Mahmassani 10 (AU: Name cited in text but not in reference list, please suggest)
Maputo Protocol 103
mediation process 58
Mexico–US relations 3–4
MIGA, *see* Multilateral Investment Guarantee Agency (MIGA)

Mike Campbell (Pvt) Ltd and Others v Zimbabwe 42
Mineral Development Agreement (MDA) 92–4
Mines and Minerals Act (1995) 100, 121
Mines and Minerals Development Act (2008) 122
Minimum Employee Benefits 116, 118
Ministry of Gender and Child Development 104n30, 113
Mittal Steel Holdings AG–Government of Liberia, MDA 92–4
Movement for Multi-party Democracy (MMD) government 111
Multilateral Investment Guarantee Agency (MIGA) 6, 9, 11, 127; Convention Establishing the Multilateral Investment Guarantee Agency 51
multilateral trade agreements 9
multilateral treaties 51–7, 127

NAFTA, *see* North American Free Trade Area (NAFTA)
national development, permanent sovereignty and 35–6
National Gender Policy (NGP) 104, 115
nationalization 3, 6; illegal 41, 42; for public purpose 41
National Transitional Government of Liberia (NTGL) 92
Nawakwi, Edith 122
Netherlands-Poland BIT, Article 3.5 of 54
New York Convention 9, 10, 58
Noble Ventures v Romania 54
non-commercial risks 6–8
North American Free Trade Agreement, Article 1110 52
North American Free Trade Area (NAFTA) 9

obsolescing bargaining model 8, 48
Overseas Private Investment Corporation (OPIC) 9, 51, 127

pacta sunt servanda 27n69, 53, 63, 66, 71
Pan American Energy LLC and BP Argentina Exploration Company v Argentina 57
Permanent Court of International Justice (PCIJ) 41, 42, 87
political risk insurance 50, 51
political risk mitigation 14, 46–7, 127; bilateral and multilateral treaties 51–7; dispute settlement clause 58–9; insurances and 50, 51; resource nationalism cycle and 47–50; stabilization clauses 59–60
preferential tax regimes 7
principle of permanent sovereignty over natural resources 4–5, 5n19, 14, 17–18, 43–4, 126–7; Charter, adoption of 20; duty to exercise permanent sovereignty for national development 35–6; duty to pay compensation 42–3; duty to respect the rights and interests of indigenous groups 36–40; duty to treat investors in accordance with international law 40–2; General Assembly Resolutions 19, 126; and International Court of Justice 23; legal status of 21–4; phases of evolution 18–21; recognition of 5; Resolution 1803 (XVII) ("landmark resolution") 18–20, 19n18; right to freely dispose of natural resources 24–8; right to freely explore and exploit natural resources 28–9; right to nationalize 32–4; right to regulate foreign investment 32; right to utilize natural resources for national development 29–31
principle of self-determination 36
principle of separability 10, 58
Protocol to the African Charter on Human and People's Rights on the Rights of Women in Africa Towards Gender Equality, *see* Maputo Protocol
public purpose 41–2, 110

rebus sic stantibus 26–7, 27n69
regional investment agreements 9
renegotiation clauses 60
replacement cost approach 81
resource nationalism cycle 7, 12, 47–50, 127; bilateral and multilateral treaties 51–7; dispute settlement clause 58–9; political risk insurance 50, 51; protections against 50–60; stabilization clauses 59–60
Revere Copper & Brass Inc. v Overseas Private Investment Corporation 73
rights under principle of permanent sovereignty 14, 126; right to freely dispose of natural resources 24–8; right to freely explore and exploit natural resources 28–9; right to regulate foreign investment 32; right to utilize natural resources for national development 29–31
Roan Selection Trust 120
Russian Revolution (1917) 3

Sabbatino v Banco Nacional de Cuba 41
SADC Protocol 103–4, 106
Salini Construttori S.P.A. and Italstrade S.P.A. v The Hashemite Kingdom of Jordan 56
Sapphire International 90
Sapphire International Petroleum Ltd. v. National Iranian Oil Co. (NIOC) 65–6, 86
Saudi Arabia v. Arabian American Oil Co. (Aramco) 67
SDGs, *see* Sustainable Development Goals (SDGs)
Section 5.5 of Seoul Declaration 32
Section 9(1) of Mines and Minerals Act (1995) 121
Section 11 of Lands Acquisition Act 120
Section 15 of GEEA 107
Section 19(1) of ZDA Act 110
Section 19(2) of Zambian Development Agency Act 8n33
Section 21 of ZDA Act 120
Section 23 of GEEA 108
Seoul Declaration 32
separability principle 10, 58
7th National Development Plan (7th NDP) 104–5, 108
SGS v Pakistan 55
SGS v Paraguay 55
SGS v Philippines 53
Sharia Law 71
Siderman de Blake v. Argentina 42
Sixth Special Session of General Assembly (1974) 20
SOABI v Senegal 90
Sornarajah, M. 33
Southern African Development Community (SADC) Protocol on Finance and Investment 9
Southern African Development Community Protocol on Gender and Development (2008), *see* SADC Protocol
Sovereign Risk Insurance Limited 51
stabilization clauses 12–13, 15, 45–6, 59–61, 77, 98, 125, 127; economic stabilization clause 62–3; effect of 63; and gender rights 128; and human rights 91–8, 128; implications of 120–3; intangibility clause 62; *stricto sensu* clause 61–2; types of 61–3; *see also* case law on stabilization clauses
Stanbic Bank 109n58
State Department of the United States 80–2
Stockholm Declaration (1972) 30
"*stricto sensu* clauses" 61–2
Study on the Problem of Discrimination Against Indigenous Populations (1971) 36
Supreme Court of Zambia 110–11
sustainability of investments 101
Sustainable Development Goals (SDGs) 100–1
Switzerland–Pakistan BIT 55
Switzerland–Paraguay BIT, Article 11 55
Switzerland–United States Treaty (1950): Article 2(3) of 2

tax stability clauses 61
Texaco Overseas Oil Petroleum Co./ California Asiatic Oil Co. v Libya 71–2
Texaco v Libya 22, 25, 26
Tippets, Abbett, McCarthy, Stratton v TAMS AFFA 33
TOTCO-Chad agreement (1998) 95
Treaty for Amazonian Co-operation (1978) 35; Article IV 28
Turkey, human rights obligations 98

UK–Egypt BIT 56
umbrella clauses, in BITs 52–7, 127
United Nations: Agenda 2030 100; Committee on the Elimination of Discrimination against Women 108
United Nations Commission on International Trade Law (UNCITRAL) Model Law on International Commercial Arbitration, Article 16(1) of 10
United Nations Convention on the Law of the Sea: Article 56(1)(a) 28; Article 193 30
United Nations Convention to Combat Desertification: Article 3(a) 39–40; Article 5(d) 40; Article 19(1)(a) 40
United Nations Fourth World Conference on Women (1995), *see* Beijing Platform
United Nations General Assembly: Resolution 275 (III) 37; Resolution 523 (VI) 19; Resolution 626 (VII) 19, 29; Resolution 1314 (XIII) 19; Resolution 1515 (XV) 19n17; Resolution 1803 (XVII) 18–20, 19n18, 29, 34, 34n97, 83, 126; Resolution 3037 (XXVII) 20; Resolution 3171 (1973) 34; Sixth Special Session (1974) 20
United Nations Mission in Liberia (UNMIL) 93

United States–Argentina BIT 56
United States–Argentina BIT 119
United States–Mexico relations 3–4
United States–Romania BIT, Article II(2)(c) 54
United States–Switzerland Treaty (1950): Article 2(3) of 2
Upton Case 42–3, 79

Velasquez Rodriguez v Honduras 119
Vienna Convention on the Law of Treaties, Article 62(1) 26–7

Washington Consensus 6
Western Sahara Case 40
Williams & Humbert v. W & T Trademarks 84
Wise v. the Attorney General 110–11
Working Group on Indigenous Populations 37
World Bank 94, 122; Guidelines on the Treatment of Foreign Direct Investment 6, 85, 85n50; investment protection 7

Zambia 13, 15–16, 124, 128; Beijing Platform in 105, 106, 113; copper mining in 99; development agreements 100, 121, 123; double taxation agreements 112; Employment Code Act, No. 3 (2019) 100, 101, 104, 116–18, 116n95, 123; Gender Equity and Equality Act (*see* Gender Equity and Equality Act (GEEA) No. 22 (2015); gender policy 101–2; Lands Acquisition Act 103, 110, 120; Mines and Minerals Act (1995) 100; mining operations, nationalization of 49; Ministry of Gender and Child Development 104n30, 113; national development plans 104–5; tax regime 122–3; *see also* gender and investment, in Zambia
Zambia Consolidated Copper Mines (ZCCM) 99, 100, 120
Zambia Development Agency (ZDA) Act 103, 110–12; Section 21 120
Zambia National Holdings and Another v the Attorney-General 120
Zambia National Holdings Limited and United National Independence Party (UNIP) v. The Attorney-General 111
Zambian Development Agency Act, Section 19(2) of 8n33
Zambia's Ministry of Gender 103

Taylor & Francis Group
an **informa** business

Taylor & Francis eBooks

www.taylorfrancis.com

A single destination for eBooks from Taylor & Francis with increased functionality and an improved user experience to meet the needs of our customers.

90,000+ eBooks of award-winning academic content in Humanities, Social Science, Science, Technology, Engineering, and Medical written by a global network of editors and authors.

TAYLOR & FRANCIS EBOOKS OFFERS:

- A streamlined experience for our library customers
- A single point of discovery for all of our eBook content
- Improved search and discovery of content at both book and chapter level

REQUEST A FREE TRIAL

support@taylorfrancis.com

Routledge
Taylor & Francis Group

CRC Press
Taylor & Francis Group